A Dictionary of

IT Service

Terms, Acronyms (

ITIL® V3 edition.

Written by:	Ashley Hanna	HP
	Ivor Macfarlane	IBM
	Stuart Rance	HP
Edited by:	Mark Lillycrop	itSMF UK
Published by:	The UK Chapter of the itSMF	

ISBN 0-9551245-7-3

Introduction

This new version of the Dictionary of IT Service Management is based on the *ITIL V3 Glossary of Terms, Definitions and Acronyms* with additional Service Management definitions provided by the authors. The Glossary is also available to download under a clickable re-use licence at www.best-management-practice.com/

Where the definition of a term includes another term, the related term is highlighted in *italics*. This is intended to help the reader with their understanding, by pointing them to additional definitions that are relevant to the original term. The form '*See also* Term X, Term Y' is used at the end of a definition where an important related term is not used within the text of the definition itself.

Terms without an asterisk (*) are taken directly from the *ITIL V3 Glossary of Terms, Definitions and Acronyms*. Other terms commonly used within IT Service Management are highlighted with an asterisk (*).

The publication names included in parentheses after the name of an ITIL V3 term identify where a reader can find more information about that term within a core ITIL V3 publication. This is either because the term is primarily used by that publication or because additional useful information about that term can be found there. Terms without a publication name associated with them may be used generally by several publications, or may not be defined in any greater detail than can be found in the glossary, i.e. we only point readers to somewhere they can expect to expand on their knowledge or to see a broader context. Terms with multiple publication names are expanded on in multiple publications.

Acceptance

Formal agreement that an *IT Service, Process, Plan*, or other *Deliverable* is complete, accurate, *Reliable* and meets its specified *Requirements*. Acceptance is usually preceded by *Evaluation* or *Testing* and is often required before proceeding to the next stage of a *Project* or *Process*.
See **Service Acceptance Criteria.**

Access Management

(Service Operation) The *Process* responsible for allowing Users to make use of *IT Services*, data, or other *Assets*. Access Management helps to protect the *Confidentiality, Integrity* and *Availability* of *Assets* by ensuring that only authorized *Users* are able to access or modify the *Assets*. Access Management is sometimes referred to as *Rights* Management or *Identity* Management.

Account Manager

(Service Strategy) A Role that is very similar to *Business Relationship Manager*, but includes more commercial aspects. Most commonly used when dealing with *External Customers*.

Accounting

(Service Strategy) The *Process* responsible for identifying actual *Costs* of delivering *IT Services*, comparing these with budgeted costs, and managing variance from the *Budget*.

Accredited

Officially authorised to carry out a *Role*. For example an Accredited body may be authorised to provide training or to conduct *Audits*.

Active Monitoring

(Service Operation) *Monitoring* of a *Configuration Item* or an *IT Service* that uses automated regular checks to discover the current status.
See **Passive Monitoring.**

Activity

A set of actions designed to achieve a particular result. Activities are usually defined as part of *Processes* or *Plans*, and are documented in *Procedures*.

Agreed Service Time

(Service Design) A synonym for *Service Hours*, commonly used in formal calculations of *Availability*. See **Downtime.**

Agreement

A *Document* that describes a formal understanding between two or more parties. An Agreement is not legally binding, unless it forms part of a *Contract*. See **Service Level Agreement, Operational Level Agreement.**

Alert

(Service Operation) A warning that a threshold has been reached, something has changed, or a *Failure* has occurred. Alerts are often created and managed by *System Management* tools and are managed by the *Event Management Process.*

Analytical Modelling

(Service Strategy) (Service Design) (Continual Service Improvement) A technique that uses mathematical *Models* to predict the behaviour of a *Configuration Item* or *IT Service*. Analytical Models are commonly used in *Capacity Management* and *Availability Management*. See **Modelling.**

Application

Software that provides *Functions* that are required by an *IT Service*. Each *Application* may be part of more than one *IT Service*. An Application runs on one or more *Servers* or *Clients*. See **Application Management, Application Portfolio.**

Application Management

(Service Design) (Service Operation) The *Function* responsible for managing *Applications* throughout their *Lifecycle*.

Application Portfolio

(Service Design) A database or structured *Document* used to manage *Applications* throughout their *Lifecycle*. The Application Portfolio contains key *Attributes* of all *Applications*. The Application Portfolio is sometimes implemented as part of the *Service Portfolio*, or as part of the *Configuration Management System*.

Application Service Provider
(ASP) (Service Design) An External Service Provider that provides IT Services using Applications running at the Service Provider's premises. Users access the Applications by network connections to the Service Provider.

Application Sizing
(Service Design) The Activity responsible for understanding the Resource Requirements needed to support a new Application, or a major Change to an existing Application. Application Sizing helps to ensure that the IT Service can meet its agreed Service Level Targets for Capacity and Performance.

Architecture
(Service Design) The structure of a System or IT Service, including the Relationships of Components to each other and to the environment they are in. Architecture also includes the Standards and Guidelines which guide the design and evolution of the System.

Assembly
(Service Transition) A Configuration Item that is made up from a number of other CIs. For example a Server CI may contain CIs for CPUs, Disks, Memory etc; an IT Service CI may contain many Hardware, Software and other CIs. See Component CI, Build.

Assessment
Inspection and analysis to check whether a Standard or set of Guidelines is being followed, that Records are accurate, or that Efficiency and Effectiveness targets are being met. See Audit.

Asset
(Service Strategy) Any Resource or Capability. Assets of a Service Provider include anything that could contribute to the delivery of a Service. Assets can be one of the following types: Management, Organisation, Process, Knowledge, People, Information, Applications, Infrastructure, and Financial Capital.

Asset Management

(*Service Transition*) Asset Management is the *Process* responsible for tracking and reporting the value and ownership of financial *Assets* throughout their *Lifecycle*. Asset Management is part of an overall *Service Asset and Configuration Management Process*.

See *Asset Register*.

Asset Register

(*Service Transition*) A list of *Assets*, which includes their ownership and value. The Asset Register is maintained by *Asset Management*.

Attribute

(*Service Transition*) A piece of information about a *Configuration Item*. Examples are name, location, *Version* number, and *Cost*. Attributes of CIs are recorded in the *Configuration Management Database (CMDB)*.

See *Relationship*.

Audit

Formal inspection and verification to check whether a *Standard* or set of *Guidelines* is being followed, that *Records* are accurate, or that *Efficiency* and *Effectiveness* targets are being met. An Audit may be carried out by internal or external groups.

See *Certification, Assessment*.

Authority Matrix

Synonym for RACI.

Automatic Call Distribution (ACD)

(*Service Operation*) Use of *Information Technology* to direct an incoming telephone call to the most appropriate person in the shortest possible time. ACD is sometimes called Automated Call Distribution.

Availability

(*Service Design*) Ability of a *Configuration Item* or *IT Service* to perform its agreed *Function* when required. Availability is determined by *Reliability, Maintainability, Serviceability, Performance*, and *Security*. Availability is usually calculated as a percentage. This calculation is often based on *Agreed Service Time* and *Downtime*. It is *Best Practice* to calculate Availability using measurements of the *Business* output of the *IT Service*.

Availability Management

(Service Design) The *Process* responsible for defining, analysing, *Planning*, measuring and improving all aspects of the *Availability* of *IT Services*. Availability Management is responsible for ensuring that all *IT Infrastructure*, *Processes*, *Tools*, *Roles* etc are appropriate for the agreed *Service Level Targets* for *Availability*.

Availability Management Information System (AMIS)

(Service Design) A virtual repository of all *Availability Management* data, usually stored in multiple physical locations.
See **Service Knowledge Management System.**

Availability Plan

(Service Design) A *Plan* to ensure that existing and future *Availability Requirements* for *IT Services* can be provided *Cost Effectively*.

Back-office / Back-end*
Business Processes or *Functions* that are not directly visible to *Business Customers*. For example order processing, shipping, receiving.
See **Front-office.**

Back-out
Synonym for *Remediation*.

Backup
(Service Design) (Service Operation) Copying data to protect against loss of *Integrity* or *Availability* of the original.

Balanced Scorecard
(Continual Service Improvement) A management tool developed by Drs. Robert Kaplan (Harvard Business School) and David Norton. A Balanced Scorecard enables a *Strategy* to be broken down into *Key Performance Indicators*. *Performance* against the *KPIs* is used to demonstrate how well the *Strategy* is being achieved. A Balanced Scorecard has 4 major areas, each of which has a small number of *KPIs*. The same 4 areas are considered at different levels of detail throughout the *Organisation*.

Baseline
(Continual Service Improvement) A *Benchmark* used as a reference point. For example:

- An *ITSM* Baseline can be used as a starting point to measure the effect of a *Service Improvement Plan*
- A *Performance* Baseline can be used to measure changes in *Performance* over the lifetime of an *IT Service*
- A *Configuration Management* Baseline can be used to enable the *IT Infrastructure* to be restored to a known *Configuration* if a *Change* or *Release* fails

Batch Processing*
Processing a set of related computer programmes, transactions or documents together as a unit. Batch Processing is often done outside of normal working hours, and may be scheduled and managed by *IT Operations Control*.

Benchmark

(Continual Service Improvement) The recorded state of something at a specific point in time. A Benchmark can be created for a *Configuration*, a *Process*, or any other set of data. For example, a benchmark can be used in:

- *Continual Service Improvement*, to establish the current state for managing improvements.
- *Capacity Management*, to document *Performance* characteristics during normal operations.

See **Benchmarking, Baseline.**

Benchmarking

(Continual Service Improvement) Comparing a *Benchmark* with a *Baseline* or with *Best Practice*. The term Benchmarking is also used to mean creating a series of *Benchmarks* over time, and comparing the results to measure progress or improvement.

Best Practice

Proven *Activities* or *Processes* that have been successfully used by multiple *Organisations*. *ITIL* is an example of Best Practice.

Brainstorming

(Service Operation) A technique that helps a team to generate ideas. Ideas are not reviewed during the Brainstorming session, but at a later stage. Brainstorming is often used by *Problem Management* to identify possible causes.

British Standards Institution (BSI)

The UK National Standards body, responsible for creating and maintaining British *Standards*. See http://www.bsi-global.com for more information. See **ISO.**

Budget

A list of all the money an *Organisation* or *Business Unit* plans to receive, and plans to pay out, over a specified period of time. See **Budgeting, Planning.**

Budgeting

The *Activity* of predicting and controlling the spending of money. Consists of a periodic negotiation cycle to set future *Budgets* (usually annual) and the day-to-day monitoring and adjusting of current *Budgets*.

Build

(Service Transition) The *Activity* of assembling a number of *Configuration Items* to create part of an *IT Service*. The term Build is also used to refer to a *Release* that is authorised for distribution. For example *Server* Build or laptop Build.

See **Configuration Baseline.**

Build Environment

(Service Transition) A controlled *Environment* where *Applications*, *IT Services* and other *Builds* are assembled prior to being moved into a *Test* or *Live Environment*.

Business

(Service Strategy) An overall corporate entity or *Organisation* formed of a number of *Business Units*. In the context of *ITSM*, the term Business includes public sector and not-for-profit organisations, as well as companies. An *IT Service Provider* provides *IT Services* to a *Customer* within a *Business*. The *IT Service Provider* may be part of the same Business as their *Customer (Internal Service Provider)*, or part of another *Business (External Service Provider)*.

Business / IT Alignment*

An approach to the delivery of *IT Services* that tries to align the *Activities* of the *IT Service Provider* with the needs of the *Business*. More recent approaches such as ITIL V3 focus on Business / IT Integration, rather than on simple alignment.

Business Capacity Management (BCM)

(Service Design) In the context of *ITSM*, Business Capacity Management is the *Activity* responsible for understanding future *Business Requirements* for use in the *Capacity Plan*.

See **Service Capacity Management.**

Business Case

(Service Strategy) Justification for a significant item of expenditure. Includes information about Costs, benefits, options, issues, *Risks*, and possible problems.

See **Cost Benefit Analysis.**

Business Continuity Management (BCM)

(Service Design) The *Business Process* responsible for managing *Risks* that could seriously impact the *Business*. BCM safeguards the interests of key stakeholders, reputation, brand and value creating activities. The BCM *Process* involves reducing *Risks* to an acceptable level and planning for the recovery of *Business Processes* should a disruption to the *Business* occur. BCM sets the *Objectives*, *Scope* and *Requirements* for *IT Service Continuity Management*.

Business Continuity Plan (BCP)

(Service Design) A *Plan* defining the steps required to *Restore Business Processes* following a disruption. The *Plan* will also identify the triggers for *Invocation*, people to be involved, communications etc. *IT Service Continuity Plans* form a significant part of *Business Continuity Plans*.

Business Continuity Plan Framework*

A template, set of guidelines, or set of outline plans used for creating multiple *Business Continuity Plans*. BCP Frameworks are most often used in organisations which need to produce plans covering many locations or business functions.

Business Customer

(Service Strategy) A recipient of a product or a *Service* from the *Business*. For example if the *Business* is a car manufacturer then the Business Customer is someone who buys a car.

Business Impact Analysis (BIA)

(Service Strategy) BIA is the *Activity* in *Business Continuity Management* that identifies *Vital Business Functions* and their dependencies. These dependencies may include *Suppliers*, people, other *Business Processes*, *IT Services* etc.

BIA defines the recovery requirements for IT Services. These requirements include *Recovery Time Objectives*, *Recovery Point Objectives* and minimum *Service Level Targets* for each *IT Service*.

Business Objective

(Service Strategy) The *Objective* of a *Business Process*, or of the *Business* as a whole. Business Objectives support the *Business Vision*, provide guidance for the *IT Strategy*, and are often supported by *IT Services*.

Business Operations
(Service Strategy) The day-to-day execution, monitoring and management of *Business Processes*.

Business Perspective
(Continual Service Improvement) An understanding of the *Service Provider* and *IT Services* from the point of view of the *Business*, and an understanding of the *Business* from the point of view of the *Service Provider*.

Business Process
A *Process* that is owned and carried out by the *Business*. A *Business Process* contributes to the delivery of a product or *Service* to a *Business Customer*. For example, a retailer may have a purchasing *Process* which helps to deliver *Services* to their *Business Customers*. Many Business Processes rely on *IT Services*.

Business Recovery*
Reinstating *Business Processes* as part of a *Business Continuity Plan*.

Business Relationship Management
(Service Strategy) The *Process* or *Function* responsible for maintaining a *Relationship* with the *Business*. BRM usually includes:
- Managing personal *Relationships* with *Business* managers
- Providing input to Service Portfolio Management
- Ensuring that the *IT Service Provider* is satisfying the *Business* needs of the *Customers*

This *Process* has strong links with *Service Level Management*.

Business Relationship Manager (BRM)
(Service Strategy) A *Role* responsible for maintaining the *Relationship* with one or more *Customers*. This *Role* is often combined with the *Service Level Manager Role*.
See **Account Manager.**

Business Representative*
Synonym for *Customer*, usually used to refer to a manager in the *Customer Organization* who is responsible for communication with the *Service Provider*.
See **Informed Customer.**

Business Service

An *IT Service* that directly supports a *Business Process*, as opposed to an *Infrastructure Service* which is used internally by the *IT Service Provider* and is not usually visible to the *Business*.

The term Business Service is also used to mean a *Service* that is delivered to *Business Customers* by *Business Units*. For example delivery of financial services to *Customers* of a bank, or goods to the *Customers* of a retail store. Successful delivery of Business Services often depends on one or more *IT Services*.

Business Service Management (BSM)

(Service Strategy) (Service Design) An approach to the management of *IT Services* that considers the *Business Processes* supported and the *Business* value provided.

This term also means the management of *Business Services* delivered to *Business Customers*.

Business Unit

(Service Strategy) A segment of the *Business* which has its own *Plans, Metrics*, income and *Costs*. Each Business Unit owns *Assets* and uses these to create value for *Customers* in the form of goods and *Services*.

Call
(Service Operation) A telephone call to the *Service Desk* from a *User*. A Call could result in an *Incident* or a *Service Request* being logged.

Call Centre
(Service Operation) An *Organisation* or *Business Unit* which handles large numbers of incoming and outgoing telephone calls.
See **Service Desk.**

Call Type
(Service Operation) A *Category* that is used to distinguish incoming requests to a *Service Desk*. Common Call Types are *Incident, Service Request* and *Complaint*.

Capability
(Service Strategy) The ability of an *Organisation*, person, *Process, Application, Configuration Item* or *IT Service* to carry out an *Activity*. *Capabilities* are intangible *Assets* of an *Organisation*.
See **Resource.**

Capability Maturity Model (CMM)
(Continual Service Improvement) The Capability Maturity Model for Software (also known as the CMM and SW-CMM) is a model used to identify *Best Practices* to help increase *Process Maturity*. CMM was developed at the Software Engineering Institute (SEI) of Carnegie Mellon University. In 2000, the SW-CMM was upgraded to *CMMI® (Capability Maturity Model Integration)*. The SEI no longer maintains the SW-CMM model, its associated appraisal methods, or training materials.

Capability Maturity Model Integration (CMMI)

(Continual Service Improvement) Capability Maturity Model® Integration (CMMI) is a process improvement approach developed by the Software Engineering Institute (SEI) of Carnegie Melon University. CMMI provides organizations with the essential elements of effective processes. It can be used to guide process improvement across a project, a division, or an entire organization. CMMI helps integrate traditionally separate organizational functions, set process improvement goals and priorities, provide guidance for quality processes, and provide a point of reference for appraising current processes. See http://www.sei.cmu.edu/cmmi/ for more information.
See ***CMM, Continuous Improvement, Maturity.***

Capacity

(Service Design) The maximum *Throughput* that a *Configuration Item* or *IT Service* can deliver whilst meeting agreed *Service Level Targets*. For some types of *CI*, Capacity may be the size or volume, for example a disk drive.

Capacity Management

(Service Design) The *Process* responsible for ensuring that the *Capacity* of *IT Services* and the *IT Infrastructure* is able to deliver agreed *Service Level Targets* in a *Cost Effective* and timely manner. Capacity Management considers all *Resources* required to deliver the IT Service, and plans for short, medium and long term *Business Requirements*.

Capacity Management Database*

A *Database* containing all data needed to support *Capacity Management*.
See ***Capacity Management Information System.***

Capacity Management Information System (CMIS)

(Service Design) A virtual repository of all *Capacity Management* data, usually stored in multiple physical locations.
See ***Service Knowledge Management System.***

Capacity Plan

(Service Design) A Capacity Plan is used to manage the *Resources* required to deliver *IT Services*. The *Plan* contains scenarios for different predictions of *Business* demand, and costed options to deliver the agreed *Service Level Targets*.

Capacity Planning
(Service Design) The *Activity* within *Capacity Management* responsible for creating a *Capacity Plan*.

Capital Expenditure (CAPEX)
(Service Strategy) The *Cost* of purchasing something that will become a financial *Asset*, for example computer equipment and buildings. The value of the *Asset* is *Depreciated* over multiple accounting periods.

Capital Item
(Service Strategy) An *Asset* that is of interest to *Financial Management* because it is above an agreed financial value.

Capitalization
(Service Strategy) Identifying major *Cost* as capital, even though no *Asset* is purchased. This is done to spread the impact of the *Cost* over multiple accounting periods. The most common example of this is software development, or purchase of a software license.

Category
A named group of things that have something in common. Categories are used to group similar things together. For example *Cost Types* are used to group similar types of *Cost*. *Incident Categories* are used to group similar types of *Incident*, CI Types are used to group similar types of *Configuration Item*.

Cause / Effect Diagram*
Synonym for *Ishikawa Diagram*.

CCTA Risk Analysis & Management Method*
See **CRAMM.**

Certification
Issuing a certificate to confirm *Compliance* to a *Standard*. Certification includes a formal *Audit* by an independent and *Accredited* body. The term Certification is also used to mean awarding a certificate to verify that a person has achieved a qualification.

Change
(Service Transition) The addition, modification or removal of anything that could have an effect on *IT Services*. The *Scope* should include all *IT Services*, *Configuration Items*, *Processes*, *Documentation* etc.

Change Advisory Board (CAB)

(Service Transition) A group of people that advises the *Change Manager* in the *Assessment*, prioritisation and scheduling of *Changes*. This board is usually made up of representatives from all areas within the *IT Service Provider*, the *Business*, and *Third Parties* such as *Suppliers*.

Change Advisory Board / Emergency Committee*

Synonym for *Emergency Change Advisory Board (ECAB)*.

Change Authority*

A *Role*, person or group that provides formal approval for a *Change*. There may be multiple Change Authorities, with different levels of approval. In many organisations a Change Manager or *Change Advisory Board (CAB)* acts as a Change Authority.

Change Case

(Service Operation) A technique used to predict the impact of proposed *Changes*. Change Cases use specific scenarios to clarify the scope of proposed *Changes* and to help with *Cost Benefit Analysis*.
See **Use Case.**

Change Control*

A limited *Change Management* process. Change Control typically includes approval of *Changes* after they have been planned and designed, but does not manage the whole *Lifecycle*.

Change History

(Service Transition) Information about all changes made to a *Configuration Item* during its life. Change History consists of all those *Change Records* that apply to the *CI*.

Change Management

(Service Transition) The *Process* responsible for controlling the *Lifecycle* of all *Changes*. The primary objective of Change Management is to enable beneficial *Changes* to be made, with minimum disruption to *IT Services*.

Change Model
(Service Transition) A repeatable way of dealing with a particular *Category* of *Change*. A Change Model defines specific pre-defined steps that will be followed for a *Change* of this *Category*. Change Models may be very simple, with no requirement for approval (e.g. Password Reset) or may be very complex with many steps that require approval (e.g. major software *Release*). See **Standard Change, Change Advisory Board.**

Change Record
(Service Transition) A *Record* containing the details of a *Change*. Each Change Record documents the *Lifecycle* of a single *Change*. A Change Record is created for every *Request for Change* that is received, even those that are subsequently rejected. Change Records should reference the *Configuration Items* that are affected by the *Change*. Change Records are stored in the *Configuration Management System*.

Change Request
Synonym for *Request for Change*.

Change Schedule
(Service Transition) A *Document* that lists all approved *Changes* and their planned implementation dates. A Change Schedule is sometimes called a Forward Schedule of Change, even though it also contains information about *Changes* that have already been implemented.

Change Slot*
Synonym for *Change Window*.

Change Window
(Service Transition) A regular, agreed time when *Changes* or *Releases* may be implemented with minimal impact on *Services*. Change Windows are usually documented in *SLAs*.

Charging
(Service Strategy) Requiring payment for *IT Services*. Charging for *IT Services* is optional, and many *Organisations* choose to treat their *IT Service Provider* as a *Cost Centre*.

Chronological Analysis
(Service Operation) A technique used to help identify possible causes of *Problems*. All available data about the *Problem* is collected and sorted by date and time to provide a detailed timeline. This can make it possible to identify which *Events* may have been triggered by others.

CI Type
(Service Transition) A *Category* that is used to Classify *CIs*. The CI Type identifies the required *Attributes* and *Relationships* for a *Configuration Record*. Common *CI Types* include: hardware, *Document*, User etc.

Classification
The act of assigning a *Category* to something. Classification is used to ensure consistent management and reporting. *CIs, Incidents, Problems, Changes* etc. are usually classified.

Client
A generic term that means a *Customer*, the *Business* or a *Business Customer*. For example Client Manager may be used as a synonym for *Account Manager*. The term client is also used to mean:
- A computer that is used directly by a *User*, for example a PC, Handheld Computer, or Workstation.
- The part of a Client-Server *Application* that the *User* directly interfaces with. For example an email Client.

Closed
(Service Operation) The final *Status* in the *Lifecycle* of an *Incident, Problem, Change* etc. When the *Status* is Closed, no further action is taken.

Closure
(Service Operation) The act of changing the *Status* of an *Incident, Problem, Change* etc. to *Closed*.

Closure Code*
A *Category* assigned to an *Incident* or *Problem* when it is *Closed*. The Closure Code typically shows the true cause or *Resolution* and is used for *Trend Analysis* and reporting.

COBIT
(Continual Service Improvement) Control Objectives for Information and related Technology (COBIT) provides guidance and *Best Practice* for the management of *IT Processes*. COBIT is published by the IT Governance Institute.
See *http://www.isaca.org/ for more information.*

Code of Practice
A *Guideline* published by a public body or a *Standards Organisation*, such as *ISO* or *BSI*. Many *Standards* consist of a Code of Practice and a *Specification*. The Code of Practice describes recommended *Best Practice*.

Cold Standby
Synonym for *Gradual Recovery*.

Commercial off the Shelf (COTS)
(Service Design) *Application* software or *Middleware* that can be purchased from a *Third Party*.

Compliance
Ensuring that a *Standard* or set of *Guidelines* is followed, or that proper, consistent accounting or other practices are being employed.

Component
A general term that is used to mean one part of something more complex. For example, a computer *System* may be a component of an *IT Service*, an *Application* may be a Component of a *Release Unit*. Components that need to be managed should be *Configuration Items*.

Component Capacity Management (CCM)
(Service Design) (Continual Service Improvement) The *Process* responsible for understanding the *Capacity*, *Utilisation*, and *Performance* of *Configuration Items*. Data is collected, recorded and analysed for use in the *Capacity Plan*.
See *Service Capacity Management.*

Component CI
(Service Transition) A *Configuration Item* that is part of an *Assembly*. For example, a CPU or Memory CI may be part of a Server CI.

Component Failure Impact Analysis (CFIA)

(Service Design) A technique that helps to identify the impact of *CI* failure on *IT Services*. A matrix is created with *IT Services* on one edge and *CIs* on the other. This enables the identification of critical *CIs* (that could cause the failure of multiple *IT Services*) and of fragile *IT Services* (that have multiple *Single Points of Failure*).

Computer Telephony Integration (CTI)

(Service Operation) CTI is a general term covering any kind of integration between computers and telephone *Systems*. It is most commonly used to refer to *Systems* where an *Application* displays detailed screens relating to incoming or outgoing telephone calls.
See *Automatic Call Distribution, Interactive Voice Response.*

Concurrency

A measure of the number of *Users* engaged in the same *Operation* at the same time.

Confidentiality

(Service Design) A security principle that requires that data should only be accessed by authorised people.

Configuration

(Service Transition) A generic term, used to describe a group of *Configuration Items* that work together to deliver an *IT Service*, or a recognisable part of an *IT Service*. Configuration is also used to describe the parameter settings for one or more *CIs*.

Configuration Baseline

(Service Transition) A *Baseline* of a *Configuration* that has been formally agreed and is managed through the *Change Management* process. A Configuration Baseline is used as a basis for future *Builds, Releases* and *Changes*.

Configuration Control

(Service Transition) The *Activity* responsible for ensuring that adding, modifying or removing a *CI* is properly managed, for example by submitting a *Request for Change* or *Service Request*.

Configuration Identification

(Service Transition) The *Activity* responsible for collecting information about *Configuration Items* and their *Relationships*, and loading this information into the *CMDB*. Configuration Identification is also responsible for labelling the *CIs* themselves, so that the corresponding *Configuration Records* can be found.

Configuration Item (CI)

(Service Transition) Any *Component* that needs to be managed in order to deliver an *IT Service*. Information about each *CI* is recorded in a *Configuration Record* within the *Configuration Management System* and is maintained throughout its *Lifecycle* by *Configuration Management*. *CIs* are under the control of *Change Management*. *CIs* typically include *IT Services*, hardware, software, buildings, people, and formal documentation such as *Process* documentation and *SLAs*.

Configuration Management

(Service Transition) The *Process* responsible for maintaining information about *Configuration Items* required to deliver an *IT Service*, including their *Relationships*. This information is managed throughout the *Lifecycle* of the *CI*. Configuration Management is part of an overall *Service Asset* and *Configuration Management Process*.

Configuration Management Database (CMDB)

(Service Transition) A database used to store *Configuration Records* throughout their *Lifecycle*. The *Configuration Management System* maintains one or more CMDBs, and each CMDB stores *Attributes* of *CIs*, and *Relationships* with other *CIs*.

Configuration Management System (CMS)

(Service Transition) A set of tools and databases that are used to manage an *IT Service Provider's Configuration* data. The CMS also includes information about *Incidents, Problems, Known Errors, Changes* and *Releases*; and may contain data about employees, *Suppliers*, locations, *Business Units, Customers* and *Users*. The CMS includes tools for collecting, storing, managing, updating, and presenting data about all *Configuration Items* and their *Relationships*. The CMS is maintained by *Configuration Management* and is used by all *IT Service Management Processes*.
See **Configuration Management Database, Service Knowledge Management System.**

Configuration Record
(Service Transition) A *Record* containing the details of a *Configuration Item*. Each Configuration Record documents the *Lifecycle* of a single *CI*. Configuration Records are stored in a *Configuration Management Database*.

Configuration Structure
(Service Transition) The hierarchy and other *Relationships* between all the *Configuration Items* that comprise a *Configuration*.

Configuration Verification*
Activities that verify configuration data is accurate.
See **Verification and Audit.**

Contingency Planning*
Planning to deal with specific risks. Contingency Planning may be included in any *Process, Activity* or *Plan*, but is most often seen as part of *Risk Management* and *IT Service Continuity Management*.

Continual Service Improvement (CSI)
(Continual Service Improvement) A stage in the *Lifecycle* of an *IT Service* and the title of one of the Core *ITIL* books.

Continual Service Improvement is responsible for managing improvements to *IT Service Management Processes* and *IT Services*. The *Performance* of the *IT Service Provider* is continually measured and improvements are made to *Processes, IT Services* and *IT Infrastructure* in order to increase *Efficiency, Effectiveness,* and *Cost Effectiveness.*
See **Plan-Do-Check-Act.**

Continual Service Improvement Programme (CSIP)
(Continual Service Improvement) A formal *Programme* to implement and manage a *Continual Service Improvement Process.*

Continuous Availability
(Service Design) An approach or design to achieve 100% *Availability*. A Continuously Available *IT Service* has no planned or unplanned *Downtime.*

Continuous Operation
(Service Design) An approach or design to eliminate planned *Downtime* of an *IT Service*. Note that individual *Configuration Items* may be down even though the *IT Service is Available.*

Contract
A legally binding *Agreement* between two or more parties.

Contract Portfolio
(Service Strategy) A database or structured *Document* used to manage *Service Contracts* or *Agreements* between an IT Service Provider and their *Customers*. Each *IT Service* delivered to a *Customer* should have a *Contract* or other *Agreement* which is listed in the Contract Portfolio.
See **Service Portfolio, Service Catalogue.**

Control
A means of managing a *Risk*, ensuring that a *Business Objective* is achieved, or ensuring that a *Process* is followed. Example Controls include *Policies, Procedures, Roles,* RAID, door-locks etc. A control is sometimes called a *Countermeasure* or safeguard.

Control also means to manage the utilization or behaviour of a *Configuration Item, System* or *IT Service.*

Control Objectives for Information and related Technology (COBIT)
See **COBIT.**

Control perspective
(Service Strategy) An approach to the management of *IT Services, Processes, Functions, Assets* etc. There can be several different Control Perspectives on the same *IT Service, Process* etc., allowing different individuals or teams to focus on what is important and relevant to their specific *Role*. Example Control Perspectives include Reactive and Proactive management within *IT Operations*, or a *Lifecycle* view for an *Application Project* team.

Control Processes
The *ISO/IEC 20000 Process* group that includes *Change Management* and *Configuration Management*.

Core Service
(Service Strategy) An *IT Service* that delivers basic *Outcomes* desired by one or more *Customers*.
See **Supporting Service, Core Service Package.**

Core Service Package (CSP)

(Service Strategy) A detailed description of a *Core Service* that may be shared by two or more *Service Level Packages*.

See **Service Package.**

Cost

The amount of money spent on a specific *Activity*, *IT Service*, or *Business Unit*. Costs consist of real cost (money), notional cost such as people's time, and *Depreciation*.

Cost Benefit Analysis

An *Activity* that analyses and compares the *Costs* and the benefits involved in one or more alternative courses of action.

See **Business Case, Net Present Value, Internal Rate of Return, Return on Investment, Value on Investment.**

Cost Centre

(Service Strategy) A *Business Unit* or *Project* to which *Costs* are assigned. A Cost Centre does not charge for *Services* provided. An *IT Service Provider* can be run as a Cost Centre or a *Profit Centre*.

Cost Effectiveness

A measure of the balance between the *Effectiveness* and *Cost* of a *Service*, *Process* or activity. A Cost Effective *Process* is one which achieves its *Objectives* at minimum *Cost*.

See **KPI, Return on Investment, Value for Money.**

Cost Element

(Service Strategy) The middle level of category to which *Costs* are assigned in *Budgeting* and *Accounting*. The highest level category is *Cost Type*. For example a *Cost Type* of "people" could have cost elements of payroll, staff benefits, expenses, training, overtime etc. Cost Elements can be further broken down to give *Cost Units*. For example the Cost Element "expenses" could include *Cost Units* of Hotels, Transport, Meals etc.

Cost Management

(Service Strategy) A general term that is used to refer to *Budgeting* and *Accounting*, sometimes used as a synonym for *Financial Management*.

Cost Type

(Service Strategy) The highest level of category to which *Costs* are assigned in *Budgeting* and *Accounting*. For example hardware, software, people, accommodation, external and *Transfer*.

See **Cost Element, Cost Type.**

Cost Unit

(Service Strategy) The lowest level of category to which *Costs* are assigned, Cost Units are usually things that can be easily counted (e.g. staff numbers, software licences) or things easily measured (e.g. CPU usage, Electricity consumed). Cost Units are included within *Cost Elements*. For example a *Cost Element* of "expenses" could include *Cost Units* of Hotels, Transport, Meals etc.

See **Cost Type.**

Countermeasure

Can be used to refer to any type of *Control*. The term Countermeasure is most often used when referring to measures that increase *Resilience*, *Fault Tolerance* or *Reliability* of an *IT Service*.

Course Corrections

Changes made to a *Plan* or *Activity* that has already started, to ensure that it will meet its *Objectives*. Course corrections are made as a result of *Monitoring* progress.

CRAMM

A methodology and tool for analysing and managing *Risks*. CRAMM was developed by the UK Government, but is now privately owned.

Further information is available from http://www.cramm.com/

Crisis Management

The *Process* responsible for managing the wider implications of *Business Continuity*. A Crisis Management team is responsible for *Strategic* issues such as managing media relations and shareholder confidence, and decides when to invoke *Business Continuity Plans*.

Critical Success Factor (CSF)

Something that must happen if a *Process, Project, Plan,* or *IT Service* is to succeed. *KPIs* are used to measure the achievement of each CSF. For example a CSF of "protect *IT Services* when making Changes" could be measured by *KPIs* such as "percentage reduction of unsuccessful *Changes*", "percentage reduction in *Changes* causing *Incidents*" etc.

Culture

A set of values that is shared by a group of people, including expectations about how people should behave, ideas, beliefs, and practices.
See **Vision.**

Customer

Someone who buys goods or *Services.* The Customer of an *IT Service Provider* is the person or group who defines and agrees the *Service Level Targets.* The term Customers is also sometimes informally used to mean *Users,* for example "this is a *Customer* focussed *Organisation*".

Customer Portfolio

(Service Strategy) A database or structured *Document* used to record all *Customers* of the *IT Service Provider.* The Customer Portfolio is the *Business Relationship Manager's* view of the *Customers* who receive *Services* from the *IT Service Provider.*
See **Contract Portfolio, Service Portfolio.**

Customer Relationship Management*

Synonym for *Business Relationship Management.*

D

Dashboard
(Service Operation) A graphical representation of overall *IT Service Performance* and *Availability*. Dashboard images may be updated in real-time, and can also be included in management reports and web pages. Dashboards can be used to support *Service Level Management*, *Event Management* or *Incident Diagnosis*.

Data-to-Information-to-Knowledge-to-Wisdom (DIKW)
A way of understanding the relationships between data, information, knowledge, and wisdom. DIKW shows how each of these builds on the others.

Definitive Hardware Store*
Synonym for *Spares Store*.

Definitive Media Library (DML)
(Service Transition) One or more locations in which the definitive and approved versions of all software *Configuration Items* are securely stored. The DML may also contain associated *CIs* such as licenses and documentation. The DML is a single logical storage area even if there are multiple locations. All software in the DML is under the control of *Change* and *Release Management* and is recorded in the *Configuration Management System*. Only software from the DML is acceptable for use in a *Release*.

Definitive Software Library*
Synonym for *Definitive Media Library (DML)*.

Deliverable
Something that must be provided to meet a commitment in a *Service Level Agreement* or a *Contract*. Deliverable is also used in a more informal way to mean a planned output of any *Process*.

Demand Management
Activities that understand and influence *Customer* demand for *Services* and the provision of *Capacity* to meet these demands. At a *Strategic* level Demand Management can involve analysis of *Patterns of Business Activity* and *User Profiles*. At a *Tactical* level it can involve use of *Differential Charging* to encourage *Customers* to use *IT Services* at less busy times.
See **Capacity Management**.

Deming Cycle
Synonym for *Plan Do Check Act*.

Dependency
The direct or indirect reliance of one *Process* or *Activity* upon another.

Deployment
(Service Transition) The *Activity* responsible for movement of new or changed hardware, software, documentation, *Process*, etc to the *Live Environment*. Deployment is part of the *Release and Deployment Management Process*.
See **Rollout.**

Depreciation
(Service Strategy) A measure of the reduction in value of an *Asset* over its life. This is based on wearing out, consumption or other reduction in the useful economic value.

Design
(Service Design) An *Activity* or *Process* that identifies *Requirements* and then defines a solution that is able to meet these *Requirements*.
See **Service Design.**

Detection
(Service Operation) A stage in the *Incident Lifecycle*. Detection results in the *Incident* becoming known to the *Service Provider*. Detection can be automatic, or can be the result of a *User* logging an *Incident*.

Development
(Service Design) The *Process* responsible for creating or modifying an *IT Service* or *Application*. Also used to mean the *Role* or group that carries out Development work.

Development Environment
(Service Design) An *Environment* used to create or modify *IT Services* or *Applications*. Development Environments are not typically subjected to the same degree of control as *Test Environments* or *Live Environments*.
See **Development.**

Diagnosis

(Service Operation) A stage in the *Incident* and *Problem Lifecycles*. The purpose of Diagnosis is to identify a *Workaround* for an *Incident* or the *Root Cause* of a *Problem*.

Diagnostic Script

(Service Operation) A structured set of questions used by *Service Desk* staff to ensure they ask the correct questions, and to help them *Classify, Resolve* and assign *Incidents*. Diagnostic Scripts may also be made available to *Users* to help them diagnose and resolve their own *Incidents*.

Differential Charging

A technique used to support *Demand Management* by charging different amounts for the same *IT Service Function* at different times.

Direct Cost

(Service Strategy) A cost of providing an *IT Service* which can be allocated in full to a specific *Customer, Cost Centre, Project* etc. For example cost of providing non-shared servers or software licenses.
See **Indirect Cost.**

Directory Service

(Service Operation) An *Application* that manages information about *IT Infrastructure* available on a network, and corresponding *User* access *Rights*.

Disaster Recovery*

Synonym for *IT Service Continuity Management*.

Do Nothing

(Service Design) A *Recovery Option*. The *Service Provider* formally agrees with the *Customer* that *Recovery* of this *IT Service* will not be performed.

Document

Information in readable form. A Document may be paper or electronic. For example a *Policy* statement, *Service Level Agreement, Incident Record*, diagram of computer room layout.
See **Record.**

Dormant Contract*

A *Contract* with a *Supplier* to provide required products or *Services* within agreed times at an agreed price. The *Contract* is invoked as part of a *Recovery Plan*, at which time an additional payment is made and the goods or *Service* are provided.

Downtime

(Service Design) (Service Operation) The time when a *Configuration Item* or *IT Service* is not *Available* during its *Agreed Service Time*. The *Availability* of an *IT Service* is often calculated from *Agreed Service Time* and Downtime.

Driver

Something that influences *Strategy*, *Objectives* or *Requirements*. For example new legislation or the actions of competitors.

Duplex*

An *Availability Management* technique. Two, usually identical, components are used, each of which is capable of performing the full task if the other fails. See **Fault Tolerance.**

Early Life Support
(Service Transition) Support provided for a new or *Changed IT Service* for a period of time after it is *Released*. During Early Life Support the *IT Service Provider* may review the *KPIs*, *Service Levels* and *Monitoring Thresholds*, and provide additional *Resources* for *Incident and Problem Management*.

ECAB
(Service Transition) A sub-set of the *Change Advisory Board* who make decisions about high impact *Emergency Changes*. Membership of the ECAB may be decided at the time a meeting is called, and depends on the nature of the *Emergency Change*.

Economies of scale
(Service Strategy) The reduction in average Cost that is possible from increasing the usage of an *IT Service* or *Asset*.
See *Economies of Scope.*

Economies of scope
(Service Strategy) The reduction in *Cost* that is allocated to an *IT Service* by using an existing *Asset* for an additional purpose. For example delivering a new *IT Service* from existing *IT Infrastructure*.
See *Economies of Scale.*

Effectiveness
(Continual Service Improvement) A measure of whether the *Objectives* of a *Process, Service* or *Activity* have been achieved. An Effective *Process* or *Activity* is one that achieves its agreed *Objectives*.
See *KPI.*

Efficiency
(Continual Service Improvement) A measure of whether the right amount of resources have been used to deliver a *Process, Service* or *Activity*. An Efficient *Process* achieves its *Objectives* with the minimum amount of time, money, people or other resources.
See *KPI.*

Emergency Change

(Service Transition) A *Change* that must be introduced as soon as possible. For example to resolve a *Major Incident* or implement a *Security* patch. The *Change Management Process* will normally have a specific *Procedure* for handling Emergency Changes.

See **Emergency Change Advisory Board (ECAB).**

End-User*

Synonym for *User*.

Environment

(Service Transition) A subset of the *IT Infrastructure* that is used for a particular purpose. For Example: *Live Environment, Test Environment, Build Environment*. It is possible for multiple Environments to share a *Configuration Item*, for example *Test* and *Live Environments* may use different partitions on a single mainframe computer. Also used in the term Physical Environment to mean the accommodation, air conditioning, power system etc.

Environment is also used as a generic term to mean the external conditions that influence or affect something.

Error

(Service Operation) A design flaw or malfunction that causes a *Failure* of one or more *Configuration Items* or *IT Services*. A mistake made by a person or a faulty *Process* that impacts a *CI* or *IT Service* is also an Error.

Escalation

(Service Operation) An *Activity* that obtains additional *Resources* when these are needed to meet *Service Level Targets* or *Customer* expectations. Escalation may be needed within any *IT Service Management Process*, but is most commonly associated with *Incident Management*, *Problem Management* and the management of *Customer* complaints. There are two types of Escalation, *Functional Escalation* and *Hierarchic Escalation*.

eSourcing Capability Model for Client Organizations (eSCM-CL)

(Service Strategy) A framework to help *Organisations* guide their analysis and decisions on *Service Sourcing Models* and *Strategies*. eSCM-CL was developed by Carnegie Mellon University.

See **eSCM-SP.**

eSourcing Capability Model for Service Providers (eSCM-SP)

(Service Strategy) A framework to help *IT Service Providers* develop their *IT Service Management Capabilities* from a *Service Sourcing* perspective. eSCM-SP was developed by Carnegie Mellon University.
See *eSCM-CL.*

Estimation

The use of experience to provide an approximate value for a *Metric* or *Cost*. Estimation is also used in *Capacity* and *Availability Management* as the cheapest and least accurate *Modelling* method.

Evaluation

(Service Transition) The *Process* responsible for assessing a new or *Changed IT Service* to ensure that *Risks* have been managed and to help determine whether to proceed with the *Change*.

Evaluation is also used to mean comparing an actual *Outcome* with the intended *Outcome*, or comparing one alternative with another.

Event

(Service Operation) A change of state which has significance for the management of a *Configuration Item* or *IT Service*.

The term Event is also used to mean an *Alert* or notification created by any *IT Service, Configuration Item* or *Monitoring* tool. Events typically require *IT Operations* personnel to take actions, and often lead to *Incidents* being logged.

Event Management

(Service Operation) The *Process* responsible for managing *Events* throughout their *Lifecycle*. Event Management is one of the main *Activities* of *IT Operations*.

Exception Report

A *Document* containing details of one or more *KPIs* or other important targets that have exceeded defined *Thresholds*. Examples include *SLA* targets being missed or about to be missed, and a *Performance Metric* indicating a potential *Capacity* problem.

Expanded Incident Lifecycle

(Availability Management) Detailed stages in the *Lifecycle* of an *Incident*. The stages are *Detection, Diagnosis, Repair, Recovery, Restoration*. The Expanded Incident Lifecycle is used to help understand all contributions to the *Impact* of *Incidents* and to *Plan* how these could be controlled or reduced.

External Customer

A *Customer* who works for a different *Business* to the *IT Service Provider*.
See **External Service Provider, Internal Customer.**

External Metric

A *Metric* that is used to measure the delivery of *IT Service* to a *Customer*. External Metrics are usually defined in *SLAs* and reported to *Customers*.
See **Internal Metric.**

External Service Provider

(Service Strategy) An *IT Service Provider* which is part of a different *Organisation* to their *Customer*. An *IT Service Provider* may have both *Internal Customers* and *External Customers*.
See **Type III Service Provider.**

External Sourcing

Synonym for *Outsourcing*.

External Target*

See **External Metric.**

Facilities Management
(Service Operation) The *Function* responsible for managing the physical *Environment* where the *IT Infrastructure* is located. Facilities Management includes all aspects of managing the physical *Environment*, for example power and cooling, building *Access Management*, and environmental *Monitoring*.

Failure
(Service Operation) Loss of ability to Operate to *Specification*, or to deliver the required output. The term Failure may be used when referring to *IT Services, Processes, Activities, Configuration* Items etc. A *Failure* often causes an *Incident*.

Failure Modes and Effects Analysis (FMEA)
An approach to assessing the potential *Impact of Failures*. FMEA involves analysing what would happen after *Failure* of each *Configuration Item*, all the way up to the effect on the Business. FMEA is often used in *Information Security Management* and in *IT Service Continuity Planning*.

Fast Recovery
(Service Design) A *Recovery Option* which is also known as Hot Standby. Provision is made to *Recover* the *IT Service* in a short period of time, typically less than 24 hours. Fast Recovery typically uses a dedicated *Fixed Facility* with computer *Systems*, and software configured ready to run the *IT Services*. Immediate Recovery may take up to 24 hours if there is a need to *Restore* data from *Backups*.

Fault
Synonym for *Error*.

Fault Tolerance
(Service Design) The ability of an *IT Service* or *Configuration Item* to continue to *Operate* correctly after *Failure* of a *Component* part.
See **Resilience, Countermeasure.**

Fault Tree Analysis (FTA)
(Service Design) (Continual Service Improvement) A technique that can be used to determine the chain of *Events* that leads to a *Problem*. Fault Tree Analysis represents a chain of *Events* using Boolean notation in a diagram.

Financial Management
(Service Strategy) The *Function* and *Processes* responsible for managing an *IT Service Provider's Budgeting, Accounting* and *Charging Requirements.*

First Level Support *
Synonym for *First-Line Support.*

First Time Fix Rate*
A *Metric* that measures the percentage of Incidents that are *Resolved* during the initial *User* contact.

First-line Support
(Service Operation) The first level in a hierarchy of *Support Groups* involved in the resolution of *Incidents.* Each level contains more specialist skills, or has more time or other *Resources.*
See **Escalation.**

Fishbone Diagram
Synonym for *Ishikawa Diagram.*

Fit for Purpose
An informal term used to describe a *Process, Configuration Item, IT Service* etc. that is capable of meeting its *Objectives* or *Service Levels.* Being Fit for Purpose requires suitable *Design,* implementation, *Control* and maintenance.

Fixed Cost
(Service Strategy) A *Cost* that does not vary with *IT Service usage.* For example the cost of *Server* hardware.
See **Variable Cost.**

Fixed Facility
(Service Design) A permanent building, available for use when needed by an *IT Service Continuity Plan.*
See **Recovery Option, Portable Facility.**

Follow the Sun
(Service Operation) A methodology for using *Service Desks* and *Support Groups* around the world to provide seamless 24 * 7 Service. *Calls, Incidents, Problems* and *Service Requests* are passed between groups in different time zones.

Fortress Approach*

An approach to *IT Service Continuity* Management where the main focus is *Risk* prevention. A typical Fortress Approach attempts to prevent all *Major Incidents*. For example building a data centre with multiple perimeter walls and earthquake resistant construction.

Forward Schedule of Change*

Synonym for *Change Schedule*.

Front-office / Front-end*

Business Processes or *Functions* that are directly visible to *Business Customers*. For example sales or marketing.
See **Back-office.**

Fulfilment

Performing *Activities* to meet a need or *Requirement*. For example by providing a new *IT Service*, or meeting a *Service Request*.

Function

A team or group of people and the tools they use to carry out one or more *Processes* or *Activities*. For example the *Service Desk*.
The term Function also has two other meanings

- An intended purpose of a *Configuration Item, Person, Team, Process,* or *IT Service*. For example one Function of an Email *Service* may be to store and forward outgoing mails, one Function of a *Business Process* may be to dispatch goods to *Customers*.
- To perform the intended purpose correctly, "The computer is Functioning"

Functional Escalation

(Service Operation) Transferring an *Incident, Problem or Change* to a technical team with a higher level of expertise to assist in an *Escalation*.

G

Gap Analysis
(Continual Service Improvement) An *Activity* which compares two sets of data and identifies the differences. Gap Analysis is commonly used to compare a set of *Requirements* with actual delivery.
See **Benchmarking.**

Governance
Ensuring that *Policies* and *Strategy* are actually implemented, and that required *Processes* are correctly followed. Governance includes defining *Roles* and responsibilities, measuring and reporting, and taking actions to resolve any issues identified.

Gradual Recovery
(Service Design) A *Recovery Option* which is also known as Cold Standby. Provision is made to *Recover* the *IT Service* in a period of time greater than 72 hours. Gradual Recovery typically uses a *Portable* or *Fixed Facility* that has environmental support and network cabling, but no computer *Systems*. The hardware and software are installed as part of the *IT Service Continuity Plan*.

Guideline
A *Document* describing *Best Practice*, that recommends what should be done. Compliance to a guideline is not normally enforced.
See **Standard.**

Help Desk

(Service Operation) A point of contact for Users to log *Incidents*. A Help Desk is usually more technically focussed than a *Service Desk* and does not provide a *Single Point of Contact* for all interaction. The term Help Desk is often used as a synonym for *Service Desk*.

Hierarchic Escalation

(Service Operation) Informing or involving more senior levels of management to assist in an *Escalation*.

High Availability

(Service Design) An approach or *Design* that minimises or hides the effects of *Configuration Item* Failure on the *Users* of an *IT Service*. High Availability solutions are *Designed* to achieve an agreed level of *Availability* and make use of techniques such as *Fault Tolerance*, *Resilience* and fast *Recovery* to reduce the number of *Incidents*, and the *Impact* of *Incidents*.

Hot Standby

Synonym for *Fast Recovery* or *Immediate Recovery*.

Identity
(Service Operation) A unique name that is used to identify a *User*, person or *Role*. The Identity is used to grant Rights to that *User*, person, or *Role*. Example identities might be the username SmithJ or the *Role* "*Change* manager".

Immediate Recovery
(Service Design) A *Recovery Option* which is also known as Hot Standby. Provision is made to *Recover* the *IT Service* with no loss of *Service*. Immediate Recovery typically uses mirroring, load balancing and split site technologies.

Impact
(Service Operation) (Service Transition) A measure of the effect of an *Incident*, *Problem* or *Change* on *Business Processes*. Impact is often based on how *Service Levels* will be affected. Impact and *Urgency* are used to assign *Priority*.

Impact Code*
A *Category* used to represent *Impact*. Impact Codes may be numbers (for example 1, 2, 3) or words (for example Major, Minor, Catastrophic).

Incident
(Service Operation) An unplanned interruption to an *IT Service* or a reduction in the *Quality* of an *IT Service*. *Failure* of a *Configuration Item* that has not yet impacted *Service* is also an Incident. For example *Failure* of one disk from a mirror set.

Incident Management
(Service Operation) The *Process* responsible for managing the *Lifecycle* of all *Incidents*. The primary *Objective* of Incident Management is to return the *IT Service* to *Users* as quickly as possible.

Incident Record
(Service Operation) A *Record* containing the details of an *Incident*. Each Incident record documents the *Lifecycle* of a single *Incident*.

Indirect Cost

(Service Strategy) A *Cost* of providing an *IT Service* which cannot be allocated in full to a specific *Customer*. For example *Cost* of providing shared *Servers* or software licenses. Also known as *Overhead*.

See ***Direct Cost.***

Information and Communications Technology (ICT)*

Synonym for *Information Technology (IT)*. The term ICT is used to emphasise the importance of communication technology.

Information Security Management (ISM)

(Service Design) The *Process* that ensures the *Confidentiality, Integrity* and *Availability* of an *Organisation's Assets*, information, data and *IT Services*. Information Security Management usually forms part of an *Organisational* approach to Security Management which has a wider scope than the *IT Service Provider*, and includes handling of paper, building access, phone calls etc., for the entire *Organisation*.

Information Security Management System (ISMS)

(Service Design) The framework of *Policy, Processes, Standards, Guidelines* and tools that ensures an *Organisation* can achieve its *Information Security Management Objectives*.

Information Security Policy

(Service Design) The *Policy* that governs the *Organisation's* approach to *Information Security Management*.

Information Technology (IT)

The use of technology for the storage, communication or processing of information. The technology typically includes computers, telecommunications, *Applications* and other software. The information may include *Business* data, voice, images, video, etc. Information Technology is often used to support *Business Processes* through *IT Services*.

Informed Customer*

A manager within the *Customer Organization* who is a specialist in managing and communicating with *Service Providers*.

See ***Business Representative.***

Infrastructure Service

An *IT Service* that is not directly used by the Business, but is required by the *IT Service Provider* so they can provide other *IT Services*. For example *Directory Services*, naming services, or communication services.

Infrastructure*

Synonym for *IT Infrastructure*. The term Infrastructure is also used to refer to any shared *Resource* within any *Organisation*.

Insourcing

Synonym for *Internal Sourcing*.

Integration Testing*

Testing of a *Build*, *Release*, or *IT Service* to demonstrate that the parts work correctly together.

Integrity

(Service Design) A security principle that ensures data and *Configuration Items* are only modified by authorised personnel and *Activities*. Integrity considers all possible causes of modification, including software and hardware *Failure*, environmental *Events*, and human intervention.

Intelligent Customer*

Synonym for *Informed Customer*.

Interactive Voice Response (IVR)

(Service Operation) A form of *Automatic Call Distribution* that accepts *User* input, such as key presses and spoken commands, to identify the correct destination for incoming *Calls*.

Intermediate Recovery

(Service Design) A *Recovery Option* which is also known as Warm Standby. Provision is made to *Recover* the *IT Service* in a period of time between 24 and 72 hours. Intermediate Recovery typically uses a shared *Portable* or *Fixed Facility* that has computer *Systems* and network *Components*. The hardware and software will need to be configured, and data will need to be restored, as part of the *IT Service Continuity Plan*.

Internal Customer

A *Customer* who works for the same *Business* as the *IT Service Provider*. See **Internal Service Provider, External Customer**.

Internal Metric

A *Metric* that is used within the *IT Service Provider* to *Monitor* the *Efficiency*, *Effectiveness* or *Cost Effectiveness* of the *IT Service Provider's* internal *Processes*. Internal Metrics are not normally reported to the *Customer* of the *IT Service*.

See ***External Metric.***

Internal Rate of Return (IRR)

(Service Strategy) A technique used to help make decisions about *Capital Expenditure*. IRR calculates a figure that allows two or more alternative investments to be compared. A larger IRR indicates a better investment.

See ***Net Present Value, Return on Investment.***

Internal Service Provider

(Service Strategy) An *IT Service Provider* which is part of the same *Organisation* as their *Customer*. An *IT Service Provider* may have both *Internal Customers* and *External Customers*.

See ***Type I Service Provider, Type II Service Provider, Insource.***

Internal Sourcing

(Service Strategy) Using an *Internal Service Provider* to manage *IT Services*.

See ***Service Sourcing, Type I Service Provider, Type II Service Provider.***

Internal Target*

See ***Internal Metric.***

International Organization for Standardization (ISO)

The International Organization for Standardization (ISO) is the world's largest developer of *Standards*. ISO is a non-governmental organization which is a network of the national standards institutes of 156 countries.

Further information about ISO is available from http://www.iso.org/

International Standards Organisation

See ***International Organization for Standardization (ISO)***

Internet Service Provider (ISP)

An *External Service Provider* that provides access to the Internet. Most ISPs also provide other *IT Services* such as web hosting.

Invocation

(Service Design) Initiation of the steps defined in a plan. For example initiating the *IT Service Continuity Plan* for one or more *IT Services*.

Ishikawa Diagram
(Service Operation) (Continual Service Improvement) A technique that helps a team to identify all the possible causes of a *Problem*. Originally devised by Kaoru Ishikawa, the output of this technique is a diagram that looks like a fishbone.

ISO 9000
A generic term that refers to a number of international *Standards* and *Guidelines for Quality Management Systems*.
See http://www.iso.org/ for more information.
See *ISO.*

ISO 9001
An international *Standard for Quality Management Systems*.
See *ISO 9000, Standard.*

ISO/IEC 17799
(Continual Service Improvement) *ISO Code of Practice* for *Information Security Management*.
See *Standard.*

ISO/IEC 20000
ISO Specification and *Code of Practice* for *IT Service Management*. ISO/IEC 20000 is aligned with *ITIL Best Practice*.

ISO/IEC 27001
(Service Design) (Continual Service Improvement) *ISO Specification* for *Information Security Management*. The corresponding *Code of Practice* is *ISO/IEC 17799*.
See *Standard.*

IT Directorate
(Continual Service Improvement) Senior Management within a *Service Provider*, charged with developing and delivering *IT services*. Most commonly used in UK Government departments.

IT Infrastructure
All of the hardware, software, networks, facilities etc. that are required to *Develop, Test*, deliver, *Monitor, Control* or support *IT Services*. The term *IT Infrastructure* includes all of the *Information Technology* but not the associated people, *Processes* and documentation.

IT Operations
(Service Operation) *Activities* carried out by *IT Operations Control*, including Console Management, *Job Scheduling*, *Backup* and Restore, and Print and Output Management.

IT Operations is also used as a synonym for *Service Operation*.

IT Operations Control
(Service Operation) The *Function* responsible for *Monitoring* and *Control* of the *IT Services* and *IT Infrastructure*.
See **Operations Bridge.**

IT Operations Management
(Service Operation) The *Function* within an *IT Service Provider* which performs the daily *Activities* needed to manage *IT Services* and the supporting *IT Infrastructure*. IT Operations Management includes *IT Operations Control* and *Facilities Management*.

IT Service
A *Service* provided to one or more *Customers* by an *IT Service Provider*. An IT Service is based on the use of *Information Technology* and supports the *Customer's Business Processes*. An *IT Service* is made up from a combination of people, *Processes* and technology and should be defined in a *Service Level Agreement*.

IT Service Continuity Management (ITSCM)
(Service Design) The *Process* responsible for managing *Risks* that could seriously impact *IT Services*. ITSCM ensures that the *IT Service Provider* can always provide minimum agreed *Service Levels*, by reducing the *Risk* to an acceptable level and *Planning for the Recovery of IT Services*. ITSCM should be designed to support *Business Continuity Management*.

IT Service Continuity Plan
(Service Design) A *Plan* defining the steps required to *Recover* one or more *IT Services*. The *Plan* will also identify the triggers for *Invocation*, people to be involved, communications etc. The IT Service Continuity Plan should be part of a *Business Continuity Plan*.

IT Service Management (ITSM)

The implementation and management of *Quality IT Services* that meet the needs of the *Business*. IT Service Management is performed by *IT Service Providers* through an appropriate mix of people, *Process* and *Information Technology*.

See **Service Management.**

IT Service Management Forum (itSMF)

The IT Service Management Forum is an independent *Organisation* dedicated to promoting a professional approach to *IT Service Management*. The itSMF is a not-for-profit membership *Organisation* with representation in many countries around the world (itSMF Chapters). The itSMF and its membership contribute to the development of *ITIL* and associated *IT Service Management Standards.*

See **http://www.itsmf.com/ for more information.**

IT Service Provider

(Service Strategy) A *Service Provider* that provides *IT Services* to *Internal Customers* or *External Customers*.

IT Steering Group (ISG)

A formal group that is responsible for ensuring that *Business* and *IT Service Provider Strategies* and *Plans* are closely aligned. An IT Steering Group includes senior representatives from the *Business* and the *IT Service Provider*.

ITIL

A set of *Best Practice* guidance for *IT Service Management*. ITIL is owned by the *OGC* and consists of a series of publications giving guidance on the provision of *Quality IT Services*, and on the *Processes* and *facilities* needed to support them.

See **http://www.itil.co.uk/ for more information.**

Job Description

A *Document* which defines the *Roles*, responsibilities, skills and knowledge required by a particular person. One Job Description can include multiple *Roles*, for example the *Roles* of *Configuration Manager* and *Change Manager* may be carried out by one person.

Job Scheduling

(Service Operation) *Planning* and managing the execution of software tasks that are required as part of an *IT Service*. Job Scheduling is carried out by *IT Operations Management*, and is often automated using software tools that run batch or online tasks at specific times of the day, week, month or year.

Kano Model

(Service Strategy) A *Model* developed by Noriaki Kano that is used to help understand *Customer* preferences. The Kano Model considers *Attributes* of an *IT Service* grouped into areas such as Basic Factors, Excitement Factors, Performance Factors etc.

Kepner & Tregoe Analysis

(Service Operation) (Continual Service Improvement) A structured approach to *Problem* solving. The *Problem* is analysed in terms of what, where, when and extent. Possible causes are identified. The most probable cause is tested. The true cause is verified.

Key Performance Indicator (KPI)

(Continual Service Improvement) A *Metric* that is used to help manage a *Process*, *IT Service* or *Activity*. Many *Metrics* may be measured, but only the most important of these are defined as KPIs and used to actively manage and report on the *Process*, *IT Service* or *Activity*. KPIs should be selected to ensure that *Efficiency*, *Effectiveness*, and *Cost Effectiveness* are all managed. See **Critical Success Factor.**

Knowledge Base

(Service Transition) A logical database containing the data used by the *Service Knowledge Management System.*

Knowledge Management

(Service Transition) The *Process* responsible for gathering, analysing, storing and sharing knowledge and information within an *Organisation*. The primary purpose of Knowledge Management is to improve *Efficiency* by reducing the need to rediscover knowledge.
See **Data-to-Information-to-Knowledge-to-Wisdom, Service Knowledge Management System.**

Known Error

(Service Operation) A *Problem* that has a documented *Root Cause* and a *Workaround*. Known Errors are created and managed throughout their *Lifecycle* by *Problem Management*. Known Errors may also be identified by *Development* or *Suppliers*.

Known Error Database (KEDB)
(Service Operation) A database containing all *Known Error Records*. This database is created by *Problem Management* and used by *Incident* and *Problem Management*. The Known Error Database is part of the *Service Knowledge Management System*.

Known Error Record
(Service Operation) A *Record* containing the details of a *Known Error*. Each Known Error Record documents the *Lifecycle* of a *Known Error*, including the *Status*, *Root Cause* and *Workaround*. In some implementations a *Known Error* is documented using additional fields in a *Problem Record*.

Lifecycle

The various stages in the life of an *IT Service, Configuration Item, Incident, Problem, Change* etc. The Lifecycle defines the *Categories* for *Status* and the *Status* transitions that are permitted. For example:

- The Lifecycle of an Application includes *Requirements, Design, Build, Deploy, Operate, Optimise.*
- The Expanded Incident Lifecycle includes Detect, Respond, Diagnose, Repair, Recover, Restore.
- The lifecycle of a Server may include: Ordered, Received, In *Test, Live,* Disposed etc.

Line of Service (LOS)

(Service Strategy) A *Core Service* or *Supporting Service* that has multiple *Service Level Packages*. A line of Service is managed by a Product Manager and each *Service Level Package* is designed to support a particular market segment.

Live

(Service Transition) Refers to an *IT Service* or *Configuration* Item that is being used to deliver *Service* to a *Customer*.

Live Environment

(Service Transition) A controlled *Environment* containing *Live Configuration Items* used to deliver *IT Services* to *Customers*.

M

Maintainability
(Service Design) A measure of how quickly and *Effectively* a *Configuration Item* or *IT Service* can be restored to normal working after a *Failure*. Maintainability is often measured and reported as *MTRS*.

Maintainability is also used in the context of *Software* or *IT Service Development* to mean ability to be *Changed* or *Repaired* easily.

Major Incident
(Service Operation) The highest *Category* of *Impact* for an *Incident*. A Major Incident results in significant disruption to the *Business*.

Managed Services
(Service Strategy) A perspective on *IT Services* which emphasises the fact that they are managed. The term Managed Services is also used as a synonym for *Outsourced IT Services*.

Management Information
Information that is used to support decision making by managers. Management Information is often generated automatically by tools supporting the various *IT Service Management Processes*. Management Information often includes the values of *KPIs* such as "Percentage of *Changes* leading to *Incidents*", or "first time fix rate".

Management of Risk (MoR)
The *OGC* methodology for managing Risks. MoR includes all the *Activities* required to identify and *Control* the exposure to *Risk* which may have an impact on the achievement of an *Organisation's Business Objectives*.
See ***http://www.m-o-r.org/ for more details.***

Management System
The framework of *Policy*, *Processes* and *Functions* that ensures an *Organisation* can achieve its *Objectives*.

Manual Workaround

A *Workaround* that requires manual intervention. Manual Workaround is also used as the name of a *Recovery Option* in which The *Business Process Operates* without the use of *IT Services*. This is a temporary measure and is usually combined with another *Recovery Option*.

Marginal Cost

(Service Strategy) The *Cost* of continuing to provide the *IT Service*. Marginal Cost does not include investment already made, for example the cost of developing new software and delivering training.

Market Space

(Service Strategy) All opportunities that an *IT Service Provider* could exploit to meet business needs of *Customers*. The Market Space identifies the possible *IT Services* that an *IT Service Provider* may wish to consider delivering.

Maturity

(Continual Service Improvement) A measure of the *Reliability, Efficiency* and *Effectiveness* of a *Process, Function, Organisation* etc. The most mature *Processes* and *Functions* are formally aligned to *Business Objectives* and *Strategy*, and are supported by a framework for continual improvement.

Maturity Level

A named level in a *Maturity* model such as the Carnegie Mellon *Capability Maturity Model Integration*.

Mean Time Between Failures (MTBF)

(Service Design) A *Metric* for measuring and reporting Reliability. MTBF is the average time that a *Configuration Item* or *IT Service* can perform its agreed *Function* without interruption. This is measured from when the *CI* or *IT Service* starts working, until it next fails.

Mean Time Between Service Incidents (MTBSI)

(Service Design) A *Metric* used for measuring and reporting *Reliability*. MTBSI is the mean time from when a *System* or *IT Service* fails, until it next fails. MTBSI is equal to *MTBF + MTRS*.

Mean Time To Repair (MTTR)

The average time taken to repair a *Configuration Item* or *IT Service* after a *Failure*. MTTR is measured from when the *CI* or *IT Service* fails until it is *Repaired*. MTTR does not include the time required to *Recover* or *Restore*. MTTR is sometimes incorrectly used to mean *Mean Time to Restore Service*.

Mean Time to Restore Service (MTRS)

The average time taken to *Restore* a *Configuration Item* or *IT Service* after a *Failure*. MTRS is measured from when the *CI* or *IT Service* fails until it is fully *Restored* and delivering its normal functionality.
See **Maintainability, Mean Time to Repair.**

Metric

(Continual Service Improvement) Something that is measured and reported to help manage a *Process, IT Service or Activity*.
See **KPI.**

Middleware

(Service Design) Software that connects two or more software *Components* or *Applications*. Middleware is usually purchased from a *Supplier*, rather than developed within the *IT Service Provider*.
See **Off the Shelf.**

Mission Statement

The Mission Statement of an *Organisation* is a short but complete description of the overall purpose and intentions of that *Organisation*. It states what is to be achieved, but not how this should be done.

Model

A representation of a *System, Process, IT Service, Configuration Item* etc. that is used to help understand or predict future behaviour.

Modelling

A technique that is used to predict the future behaviour of a *System, Process, IT Service, Configuration Item* etc. Modelling is commonly used in *Financial Management, Capacity Management* and *Availability Management*.

Monitor Control Loop

(Service Operation) *Monitoring* the output of a *Task, Process, IT Service* or *Configuration Item*; comparing this output to a predefined norm; and taking appropriate action based on this comparison.

Monitoring

(Service Operation) Repeated observation of a *Configuration Item, IT Service* or *Process* to detect *Events* and to ensure that the current status is known.

Near-Shore
(Service Strategy) Provision of *Services* from a country near the country where the *Customer* is based. This can be the provision of an *IT Service*, or of supporting *Functions* such as *Service Desk*.
See **On-shore, Off-shore.**

Net Present Value (NPV)
(Service Strategy) A technique used to help make decisions about *Capital Expenditure*. NPV compares cash inflows to cash outflows. Positive NPV indicates that an investment is worthwhile.
See **Internal Rate of Return, Return on Investment.**

Notional Charging
(Service Strategy) An approach to *Charging* for *IT Services*. Charges to *Customers* are calculated and *Customers* are informed of these charges, but no money is actually transferred. Notional Charging is sometimes introduced to ensure that *Customers* are aware of the *Costs* they incur, or as a stage during the introduction of real *Charging*.

O

Objective
The defined purpose or aim of a *Process*, an *Activity* or an *Organisation* as a whole. Objectives are usually expressed as measurable targets. The term Objective is also informally used to mean a *Requirement*.
See **Outcome.**

Off the Shelf
Synonym for *Commercial Off the Shelf.*

Office of Government Commerce (OGC)
OGC owns the *ITIL* brand (copyright and trademark). OGC is a UK Government department that supports the delivery of the government's procurement agenda through its work in collaborative procurement and in raising levels of procurement skills and capability with departments. It also provides support for complex public sector projects.

Office of Public Sector Information (OPSI)
OPSI license the Crown Copyright material used in the *ITIL* publications. They are a UK Government department who provide online access to UK legislation, license the re-use of Crown copyright material, manage the Information Fair Trader Scheme, maintain the Government's Information Asset Register and provide advice and guidance on official publishing and Crown copyright.

Off-shore
(Service Strategy) Provision of *Services* from a location outside the country where the *Customer* is based, often in a different continent. This can be the provision of an *IT Service*, or of supporting *Functions* such as *Service Desk*.
See **On-shore, Near-shore.**

On-shore
(Service Strategy) Provision of *Services* from a location within the country where the *Customer* is based.
See **Off-shore, Near-shore.**

Operate

To perform as expected. A *Process* or *Configuration Item* is said to Operate if it is delivering the *Required* outputs. Operate also means to perform one or more *Operations*. For example, to Operate a computer is to do the day-to-day *Operations* needed for it to perform as expected.

Operation

(Service Operation) Day-to-day management of an *IT Service, System*, or other *Configuration Item*. Operation is also used to mean any pre-defined *Activity* or *Transaction*. For example loading a magnetic tape, accepting money at a point of sale, or reading data from a disk drive.

Operational

The lowest of three levels of *Planning* and delivery (*Strategic, Tactical,* Operational). Operational *Activities* include the day-to-day or short term *Planning* or delivery of a *Business Process* or *IT Service Management Process*. The term *Operational* is also a synonym for *Live*.

Operational / Production Acceptance*

Part of *Service Acceptance* responsible for ensuring that everything needed to support a new or changed Service is in place. Operational Acceptance often uses a checklist to ensure that all required documentation, *IT Operations Processes*, tools and training are complete.

Operational Cost

Cost resulting from running the *IT Services*. Often repeating payments. For example staff costs, hardware maintenance and electricity (also known as "current expenditure" or "revenue expenditure").
See **Capital Expenditure.**

Operational Expenditure (OPEX)

Synonym for *Operational Cost*.

Operational Level Agreement (OLA)

(Service Design) (Continual Service Improvement) An *Agreement* between an *IT Service Provider* and another part of the same *Organisation*. An OLA supports the *IT Service Provider's* delivery of *IT Services* to *Customers*. The OLA defines the goods or *Services* to be provided and the responsibilities of both parties. For example there could be an OLA

- between the *IT Service Provider* and a procurement department to obtain hardware in agreed times
- between the Service Desk and a Support Group to provide Incident Resolution in agreed times.

See **Service Level Agreement.**

Operations Bridge

(Service Operation) A physical location where *IT Services* and *IT Infrastructure* are monitored and managed.

Operations Control

Synonym for *IT Operations Control.*

Operations Management

Synonym for *IT Operations Management.*

Opportunity Cost

(Service Strategy) A *Cost* that is used in deciding between investment choices. Opportunity Cost represents the revenue that would have been generated by using the *Resources* in a different way. For example the Opportunity Cost of purchasing a new *Server* may include not carrying out a *Service Improvement* activity that the money could have been spent on. Opportunity cost analysis is used as part of a decision making processes, but is not treated as an actual *Cost* in any financial statement.

Optimise

Review, Plan and request *Changes*, in order to obtain the maximum *Efficiency* and *Effectiveness* from a *Process, Configuration Item, Application* etc.

Organisation

A company, legal entity or other institution. Examples of Organisations that are not companies include *International Standards Organisation* or *itSMF*. The term Organisation is sometimes used to refer to any entity which has *People, Resources* and *Budgets*. For example a *Project* or *Business Unit*.

Outcome

The result of carrying out an *Activity*; following a *Process*; delivering an *IT Service* etc. The term Outcome is used to refer to intended results, as well as to actual results.

See *Objective.*

Outsourcing

(Service Strategy) Using an *External Service Provider* to manage *IT Services.*

See *Service Sourcing, Type III Service Provider.*

Overhead

Synonym for *Indirect cost*

Pain Factor*
Synonym for *Pain Value*.

Pain Value Analysis
(Service Operation) A technique used to help identify the *Business Impact* of one or more *Problems*. A formula is used to calculate Pain Value based on the number of *Users* affected, the duration of the *Downtime*, the *Impact* on each *User*, and the cost to the *Business* (if known).

Pareto Principle
(Service Operation) A technique used to prioritise *Activities*. The Pareto Principle says that 80% of the value of any *Activity* is created with 20% of the effort. Pareto Analysis is also used in *Problem Management* to prioritise possible Problem causes for investigation.

Partnership
A relationship between two *Organisations* which involves working closely together for common goals or mutual benefit. The *IT Service Provider* should have a Partnership with the *Business*, and with *Third Parties* who are critical to the delivery of *IT Services*.
See **Value Network.**

Passive Monitoring
(Service Operation) *Monitoring* of a *Configuration Item*, an *IT Service* or a *Process* that relies on an *Alert* or notification to discover the current status.
See **Active Monitoring.**

Pattern of Business Activity (PBA)
(Service Strategy) A *Workload* profile of one or more *Business Activities*. Patterns of Business Activity are used to help the *IT Service Provider* understand and plan for different levels of Business Activity.
See **User Profile.**

Percentage utilisation
(Service Design) The amount of time that a *Component* is busy over a given period of time. For example, if a CPU is busy for 1800 seconds in a one hour period, its utilisation is 50%

Performance

A measure of what is achieved or delivered by a *System*, person, team, *Process*, or *IT Service*.

Performance Anatomy

(Service Strategy) An approach to *Organisational Culture* that integrates, and actively manages, leadership and strategy, people development, technology enablement, performance management and innovation.

Performance Management

(Continual Service Improvement) The Process responsible for day-to-day *Capacity Management Activities*. These include *Monitoring*, *Threshold* detection, *Performance* analysis and *Tuning*, and implementing *Changes* related to *Performance* and *Capacity*.

Pilot

(Service Transition) A limited *Deployment* of an *IT Service*, a *Release* or a *Process* to the *Live Environment*. A Pilot is used to reduce *Risk* and to gain *User* feedback and *Acceptance*.
See **Test, Evaluation.**

Plan

A detailed proposal which describes the *Activities* and *Resources* needed to achieve an *Objective*. For example a *Plan* to implement a new *IT Service* or *Process*. *ISO/IEC 20000* requires a *Plan* for the management of each *IT Service Management Process*.

Plan-Do-Check-Act

(Continual Service Improvement) A four stage cycle for *Process* management, attributed to Edward Deming. Plan-Do-Check-Act is also called the *Deming Cycle*.
PLAN: *Design* or revise *Processes* that support the *IT Services*.
DO: Implement the *Plan* and manage the *Processes*.
CHECK: Measure the *Processes* and *IT Services*, compare with *Objectives* and produce reports
ACT: *Plan* and implement *Changes* to improve the *Processes*.

Planned Downtime

(Service Design) Agreed time when an *IT Service* will not be available. Planned Downtime is often used for maintenance, upgrades and testing.
See **Change Window, Downtime.**

Planning

An *Activity* responsible for creating one or more Plans. For example, *Capacity Planning*.

PMBOK

A *Project* management *Standard* maintained and published by the Project Management Institute. PMBOK stands for Project Management Body of Knowledge. See http://www.pmi.org/ for more information.
See **PRINCE2.**

Policy

Formally documented management expectations and intentions. Policies are used to direct decisions, and to ensure consistent and appropriate development and implementation of *Processes, Standards, Roles, Activities, IT Infrastructure* etc.

Portable Facility

(Service Design) A prefabricated building, or a large vehicle, provided by a *Third Party* and moved to a site when needed by an *IT Service Continuity Plan*.
See **Recovery Option, Fixed Facility.**

Post Implementation Review (PIR)

A *Review* that takes place after a *Change* or a *Project* has been implemented. A PIR determines if the *Change* or *Project* was successful, and identifies opportunities for improvement.

Practice

A way of working, or a way in which work must be done. Practices can include *Activities, Processes, Functions, Standards* and *Guidelines*.
See **Best Practice.**

Prerequisite for Success (PFS)

An *Activity* that needs to be completed, or a condition that needs to be met, to enable successful implementation of a *Plan* or *Process*. A PFS is often an output from one *Process* that is a required input to another *Process*.

Pricing

(Service Strategy) The *Activity* for establishing how much *Customers* will be *Charged*.

PRINCE2
The standard UK government methodology for *Project* management.
See ***http://www.ogc.gov.uk/prince2/ for more information.***
See ***PMBOK.***

Priority
(Service Transition) (Service Operation) A *Category* used to identify the relative importance of an *Incident, Problem* or *Change*. Priority is based on *Impact* and *Urgency*, and is used to identify required times for actions to be taken. For example the *SLA* may state that Priority2 *Incidents* must be resolved within 12 hours.

Proactive Monitoring
(Service Operation) *Monitoring* that looks for patterns of *Events* to predict possible future *Failures*.
See ***Reactive Monitoring.***

Proactive Problem Management
(Service Operation) Part of the *Problem Management Process*. The *Objective* of Proactive Problem Management is to identify *Problems* that might otherwise be missed. Proactive Problem Management analyses *Incident Records*, and uses data collected by other *IT Service Management Processes* to identify trends or significant *Problems*.

Problem
(Service Operation) A cause of one or more *Incidents*. The cause is not usually known at the time a *Problem Record* is created, and the *Problem Management Process* is responsible for further investigation.

Problem Management
(Service Operation) The *Process* responsible for managing the *Lifecycle* of all *Problems*. The primary *Objectives* of Problem Management are to prevent *Incidents* from happening, and to minimise the *Impact* of *Incidents* that cannot be prevented.

Problem Record
(Service Operation) A *Record* containing the details of a *Problem*. Each Problem Record documents the Lifecycle of a single Problem.

Procedure

A *Document* containing steps that specify how to achieve an *Activity*. Procedures are defined as part of *Processes*.

See **Work Instruction.**

Process

A structured set of *Activities* designed to accomplish a specific *Objective*. A Process takes one or more defined inputs and turns them into defined outputs. A Process may include any of the *Roles*, responsibilities, tools and management *Controls* required to reliably deliver the outputs. A Process may define *Policies, Standards, Guidelines, Activities,* and *Work Instructions* if they are needed.

Process Control

The *Activity* of planning and regulating a *Process*, with the *Objective* of performing the *Process* in an *Effective, Efficient,* and consistent manner.

Process Manager

A *Role* responsible for *Operational* management of a *Process*. The Process Manager's responsibilities include *Planning* and co-ordination of all *Activities* required to carry out, monitor and report on the *Process*. There may be several Process Managers for one *Process*, for example regional Change Managers or IT Service Continuity Managers for each data centre. The *Process Manager Role* is often assigned to the person who carries out the *Process Owner Role*, but the two *Roles* may be separate in larger *Organisations*.

Process Maturity*
See **Maturity.**

Process Owner

A *Role* responsible for ensuring that a *Process* is *Fit for Purpose*. The Process Owner's responsibilities include sponsorship, *Design, Change Management* and continual improvement of the *Process* and its *Metrics*. This *Role* is often assigned to the same person who carries out the *Process Manager Role*, but the two *Roles* may be separate in larger *Organisations*.

Production Environment

Synonym for *Live Environment*.

Profit Centre
(Service Strategy) A *Business Unit* which charges for *Services* provided. A Profit Centre can be created with the objective of making a profit, recovering *Costs*, or running at a loss. An *IT Service Provider* can be run as a *Cost Centre* or a Profit Centre.

pro-forma
A template, or example *Document* containing example data that will be replaced with the real values when these are available.

Programme
A number of *Projects* and *Activities* that are planned and managed together to achieve an overall set of related *Objectives* and other *Outcomes*.

Project
A temporary *Organisation*, with people and other *Assets* required to achieve an *Objective* or other *Outcome*. Each Project has a *Lifecycle* that typically includes *initiation*, *Planning*, execution, *Closure* etc. Projects are usually managed using a formal methodology such as *PRINCE2*.

Project Evaluation Review*
Synonym for *Post Implementation Review (PIR)*, used in the context of a completed *Project*.

Projected Service Outage (PSO)
(Service Transition) A *Document* that identifies the effect of planned *Changes*, maintenance *Activities* and *Test Plans* on agreed *Service Levels*.

PRojects IN Controlled Environments (PRINCE2)
See *PRINCE2*

Q

Qualification
(Service Transition) An *Activity* that ensures that *IT Infrastructure* is appropriate, and correctly configured, to support an *Application* or *IT Service*. See **Validation.**

Quality
The ability of a product, *Service*, or *Process* to provide the intended value. For example, a hardware *Component* can be considered to be of high *Quality* if it performs as expected and delivers the required *Reliability*. *Process Quality* also requires an ability to monitor *Effectiveness* and *Efficiency*, and to improve them if necessary.
See **Quality Management System.**

Quality Assurance (QA)
(Service Transition) The *Process* responsible for ensuring that the *Quality* of a product, *Service* or *Process* will provide its intended *Value*.

Quality Management System (QMS)
(Continual Service Improvement) The set of *Processes* responsible for ensuring that all work carried out by an *Organisation* is of a suitable *Quality* to reliably meet *Business Objectives* or *Service Levels*.
See **ISO 9000.**

Queuing Theory*
An *Analytical Modelling* technique that models the rate of arrival of requests for *Resources* such as disks, CPUs, servers, *Services* etc. Queuing Theory can be used to predict the *Response Times* and *Resource* requirements of *Systems* when the *Throughput* or *Workload* changes.

Quick Win
(Continual Service Improvement) An improvement *Activity* which is expected to provide a *Return on Investment* in a short period of time with relatively small *Cost* and effort.
See **Pareto Principle.**

RACI
(Service Design) (Continual Service Improvement) A *Model* used to help define Roles and Responsibilities. RACI stands for Responsible, Accountable, Consulted and Informed.
See *Stakeholder.*

RAG (Red Amber Green) Chart*
A type of *SLAM Chart* that uses Red, Amber and Green colours to indicate failure, warning and success states.

Reactive Monitoring
(Service Operation) *Monitoring* that takes action in response to an *Event*. For example submitting a batch job when the previous job completes, or logging an *Incident* when an *Error* occurs.
See *Proactive Monitoring.*

Reciprocal Arrangement
(Service Design) A *Recovery Option*. An agreement between two *Organisations* to share resources in an emergency. For example, *Computer Room* space or use of a mainframe.

Record
A *Document* containing the results or other output from a *Process* or *Activity*. Records are evidence of the fact that an *Activity* took place and may be paper or electronic. For example, an *Audit* report, an *Incident Record*, or the minutes of a meeting.

Recovery
(Service Design) (Service Operation) Returning a *Configuration Item* or an *IT Service* to a working state. Recovery of an *IT Service* often includes recovering data to a known consistent state. After Recovery, further steps may be needed before the *IT Service* can be made available to the *Users* (*Restoration*).

Recovery Option

(Service Design) A *Strategy* for responding to an interruption to *Service*. Commonly used *Strategies* are *Do Nothing, Manual Workaround, Reciprocal Arrangement, Gradual Recovery, Intermediate Recovery, Fast Recovery, Immediate Recovery*. Recovery Options may make use of dedicated facilities, or *Third Party* facilities shared by multiple *Businesses*.

Recovery Point Objective (RPO)

(Service Operation) The maximum amount of data that may be lost when *Service* is *Restored* after an interruption. Recovery Point Objective is expressed as a length of time before the *Failure*. For example a Recovery Point Objective of one day may be supported by daily *Backups*, and up to 24 hours of data may be lost. Recovery Point Objectives for each *IT Service* should be negotiated, agreed and documented, and used as *Requirements* for *Service Design* and *IT Service Continuity Plans*.

Recovery Time Objective (RTO)

(Service Operation) The maximum time allowed for recovery of an *IT Service* following an interruption. The *Service Level* to be provided may be less than normal *Service Level Targets*. Recovery Time Objectives for each *IT Service* should be negotiated, agreed and documented.
See **Business Impact Analysis.**

Redundancy

Synonym for *Fault Tolerance*.
The term Redundant also has a generic meaning of obsolete, or no longer needed.

Relationship

A connection or interaction between two people or things. In *Business Relationship Management* it is the interaction between the *IT Service Provider* and the *Business*. In *Configuration Management* it is a link between two *Configuration Items* that identifies a dependency or connection between them. For example *Applications* may be linked to the *Servers* they run on, *IT Services* have many links to all the *CIs* that contribute to them.

Relationship Processes

The *ISO/IEC 20000 Process* group that includes *Business Relationship Management* and *Supplier Management*.

Release
(**Service Transition**) A collection of hardware, software, documentation, *Processes* or other *Components* required to implement one or more approved *Changes* to *IT Services*. The contents of each Release are managed, *Tested*, and *Deployed* as a single entity.

Release Acceptance*
Acceptance of a *Release*, prior to *Deployment*.

Release and Deployment Management
(**Service Transition**) The Process responsible for both Release Management and Deployment.

Release Identification
(**Service Transition**) A naming convention used to uniquely identify a *Release*. The Release Identification typically includes a reference to the *Configuration Item* and a version number. For example Microsoft Office 2003 SR2.

Release Management
(**Service Transition**) The *Process* responsible for *Planning*, scheduling and controlling the movement of *Releases* to *Test* and *Live Environments*. The primary *Objective* of Release Management is to ensure that the integrity of the *Live Environment* is protected and that the correct *Components* are released. Release Management is part of the *Release and Deployment Management Process*.

Release Mechanism*
The method for deploying a *Release* to its target *Environment*. A Release Mechanism may include hardware and software tools as well as *Procedures*.

Release Process
The name used by *ISO/IEC 20000* for the *Process* group that includes *Release Management*. This group does not include any other *Processes*.

Release Process is also used as a synonym for *Release Management Process*.

Release Record
(**Service Transition**) A *Record* in the *CMDB* that defines the content of a *Release*. A *Release Record* has *Relationships* with all *Configuration Items* that are affected by the *Release*.

Release Schedule*

A *Document* that lists all *Releases* and their planned implementation details and dates. The Release Schedule is published to relevant *Stakeholders*.

Release Unit

(Service Transition) *Components* of an *IT Service* that are normally *Released* together. A Release Unit typically includes sufficient *Components* to perform a useful *Function*. For example one Release Unit could be a Desktop PC, including Hardware, Software, Licenses, Documentation etc. A different Release Unit may be the complete Payroll Application, including *IT Operations Procedures* and *User training*.

Release Window

Synonym for *Change Window*.

Reliability

(Service Design) (Continual Service Improvement) A measure of how long a *Configuration Item* or *IT Service* can perform its agreed *Function* without interruption. Usually measured as *MTBF* or *MTBSI*. The term Reliability can also be used to state how likely it is that a *Process, Function* etc. will deliver its required outputs.
See **Availability.**

Remediation

(Service Transition) *Recovery* to a known state after a failed *Change* or *Release*.

Remote Fix *

Resolution of an *Incident* or *Problem* without support staff visiting the physical location of the failed *Configuration Item*.

Repair

(Service Operation) The replacement or correction of a failed *Configuration Item*.

Request for Change (RFC)

(Service Transition) A formal proposal for a *Change* to be made. An RFC includes details of the proposed *Change*, and may be recorded on paper or electronically. The term RFC is often misused to mean a *Change Record*, or the *Change* itself.

Request for Service*
Synonym for *Service Request*.

Request Fulfilment
(Service Operation) The *Process* responsible for managing the *Lifecycle* of all *Service Requests*.

Requirement
(Service Design) A formal statement of what is needed. For example a *Service Level Requirement*, a *Project Requirement* or the required *Deliverables* for a *Process*.
See **Statement of Requirements.**

Resilience
(Service Design) The ability of a *Configuration Item* or *IT Service* to resist *Failure* or to *Recover* quickly following a *Failure*. For example, an armoured cable will resist failure when put under stress.
See **Fault Tolerance.**

Resolution
(Service Operation) Action taken to repair the *Root Cause* of an *Incident* or *Problem*, or to *implement* a *Workaround*.

In *ISO/IEC 20000*, *Resolution Processes* is the *Process* group that includes *Incident* and *Problem Management*.

Resolution Processes
The *ISO/IEC 20000 Process* group that includes *Incident Management* and *Problem Management*.

Resource
(Service Strategy) A generic term that includes *IT Infrastructure*, people, money or anything else that might help to deliver an *IT Service*. Resources are considered to be *Assets* of an *Organisation*.
See **Capability, Service Asset.**

Resource Capacity Management*
Synonym for *Component Capacity Management*.

Response Time
A measure of the time taken to complete an *Operation* or *Transaction*. Used in *Capacity Management* as a measure of *IT Infrastructure Performance*, and in *Incident Management* as a measure of the time taken to answer the phone, or to start *Diagnosis*.

Responsiveness
A measurement of the time taken to respond to something. This could be *Response Time* of a *Transaction*, or the speed with which an *IT Service Provider* responds to an *Incident* or *Request for Change* etc.

Restoration of Service
See *Restore.*

Restore
(Service Operation) Taking action to return an *IT Service* to the *Users* after *Repair* and *Recovery* from an *Incident*. This is the primary *Objective* of *Incident Management*.

Retire
(Service Transition) Permanent removal of an *IT Service*, or other *Configuration Item*, from the *Live Environment*. Retired is a stage in the *Lifecycle* of many *Configuration Items*.

Return on Investment (ROI)
(Service Strategy) (Continual Service Improvement) A measurement of the expected benefit of an investment. In the simplest sense it is the net profit of an investment divided by the net worth of the assets invested.
See *Net Present Value, Value on Investment.*

Return to Normal
(Service Design) The phase of an *IT Service Continuity Plan* during which full normal operations are resumed. For example, if an alternate data centre has been in use, then this phase will bring the primary data centre back into operation, and restore the ability to invoke IT Service Continuity Plans again.

Review

An evaluation of a *Change, Problem, Process, Project* etc. Reviews are typically carried out at predefined points in the *Lifecycle*, and especially after *Closure*. The purpose of a Review is to ensure that all *Deliverables* have been provided, and to identify opportunities for improvement.
See **Post Implementation Review.**

Rights

(Service Operation) Entitlements, or permissions, granted to a *User* or *Role*. For example the Right to modify particular data, or to authorize a *Change*.

Risk

A possible *Event* that could cause harm or loss, or affect the ability to achieve *Objectives*. A Risk is measured by the probability of a *Threat*, the *Vulnerability* of the *Asset* to that Threat, and the *Impact* it would have if it occurred.

Risk Analysis*

Synonym for *Risk Assessment*.

Risk Assessment

The initial steps of *Risk Management*. Analysing the value of *Assets* to the business, identifying *Threats* to those *Assets*, and evaluating how *Vulnerable* each *Asset* is to those *Threats*. Risk Assessment can be quantitative (based on numerical data) or qualitative.

Risk Management

The *Process* responsible for identifying, assessing and controlling *Risks*.
See **Risk Assessment.**

Risk Reduction Measure*

Action taken to reduce the likelihood or *Impact* of a Risk.
See **Control.**

Role

A set of responsibilities, *Activities* and authorities granted to a person or team. A Role is defined in a *Process*. One person or team may have multiple Roles, for example the Roles of *Configuration Manager* and *Change Manager* may be carried out by a single person.

Rollout
(Service Transition) Synonym for *Deployment*. Most often used to refer to complex or phased *Deployments* or *Deployments* to multiple locations.

Root Cause
(Service Operation) The underlying or original cause of an *Incident* or *Problem*.

Root Cause Analysis (RCA)
(Service Operation) An *Activity* that identifies the *Root Cause* of an *Incident* or *Problem*. RCA typically concentrates on *IT Infrastructure* *failures*.
See **Service Failure Analysis.**

Running Costs
Synonym for *Operational Costs*

Scalability
The ability of an *IT Service, Process, Configuration Item* etc. to perform its agreed *Function* when the *Workload* or *Scope* changes.

Scope
The boundary, or extent, to which a *Process, Procedure, Certification, Contract* etc. applies. For example the Scope of *Change Management* may include all *Live IT Services* and related *Configuration Items*, the Scope of an *ISO/IEC 20000 Certificate* may include all *IT Services* delivered out of a named data centre.

Script*
A sequence of predefined steps. For example a *Diagnostic Script*, or an automated computer Script executed as part of *System Management* or *IT Operations*.

Second Level Support *
Synonym for *Second-line Support*.

Second-line Support
(Service Operation) The second level in a hierarchy of *Support Groups* involved in the resolution of *Incidents* and investigation of *Problems*. Each level contains more specialist skills, or has more time or other *Resources*.

Security
See **Information Security Management.**

Security Management
Synonym for *Information Security Management*

Security Policy
Synonym for *Information Security Policy*

Separation of Concerns (SoC)
(Service Strategy) An approach to *Designing* a solution or *IT Service* that divides the problem into pieces that can be solved independently. This approach separates "what" is to be done from "how" it is to be done.

Server

(Service Operation) A computer that is connected to a network and provides software *Functions* that are used by other computers.

Service

A means of delivering value to *Customers* by facilitating *Outcomes Customers* want to achieve without the ownership of specific *Costs* and *Risks*.

Service Acceptance Criteria (SAC)

(Service Transition) A set of criteria used to ensure that an *IT Service* meets its functionality and *Quality Requirements* and that the *IT Service Provider* is ready to Operate the new *IT Service* when it has been *Deployed*.
See **Acceptance.**

Service Achievement*

Synonym for *Service Level*.

Service Analytics

(Service Strategy) A technique used in the Assessment of the *Business Impact* of *Incidents*. Service Analytics *Models* the dependencies between *Configuration Items*, and the dependencies of *IT Services* on *Configuration Items*.

Service Asset

Any *Capability* or *Resource* of a *Service Provider*.
See **Asset.**

Service Asset and Configuration Management (SACM)

(Service Transition) The *Process* responsible for both *Configuration Management* and *Asset Management*.

Service Capacity Management (SCM)

(Service Design) (Continual Service Improvement) The *Activity* responsible for understanding the *Performance* and *Capacity* of *IT Services*. The *Resources* used by each *IT Service* and the pattern of usage over time are collected, recorded, and analysed for use in the *Capacity Plan*.
See **Business Capacity Management, Component Capacity Management.**

Service Catalogue
(Service Design) A database or structured *Document* with information about all *Live IT Services*, including those available for *Deployment*. The Service Catalogue is the only part of the *Service Portfolio* published to *Customers*, and is used to support the sale and delivery of *IT Services*. The Service Catalogue includes information about deliverables, prices, contact points, ordering and request *Processes*.
See **Contract Portfolio.**

Service Charter*
A *Document* that defines the generic level of *Service* that a *Customer* can expect from their *Service Provider*. The Service Charter will typically include details of the *Service Providers' Mission Statement, Vision and Culture.*

Service Continuity Management
Synonym for *IT Service Continuity Management*.

Service Contract
(Service Strategy) A *Contract* to deliver one or more *IT Services*. The term Service Contract is also used to mean any *Agreement* to deliver *IT Services*, whether this is a legal *Contract* or an *SLA*.
See **Contract Portfolio.**

Service Culture
A Customer oriented *Culture*. The major *Objectives* of a Service Culture are *Customer* satisfaction and helping the Customer to achieve their *Business Objectives*.

Service Design
(Service Design) A stage in the *Lifecycle* of an *IT Service*. Service Design includes a number of *Processes* and *Functions* and is the title of one of the Core *ITIL* books.
See **Design.**

Service Design Package
(Service Design) *Document(s)* defining all aspects of an *IT Service* and its *Requirements* through each stage of its *Lifecycle*. A Service Design Package is produced for each new *IT Service*, major *Change*, or *IT Service Retirement*.

Service Desk
(Service Operation) The *Single Point of Contact* between the *Service Provider* and the *Users*. A typical Service Desk manages *Incidents* and *Service Requests*, and also handles communication with the *Users*.

Service Failure Analysis (SFA)
(Service Design) An *Activity* that identifies underlying causes of one or more *IT Service* interruptions. SFA identifies opportunities to improve the *IT Service Provider's Processes* and tools, and not just the *IT Infrastructure*. SFA is a time constrained, project-like activity, rather than an ongoing process of analysis. See **Root Cause Analysis.**

Service Hours
(Service Design) (Continual Service Improvement) An agreed time period when a particular *IT Service* should be *Available*. For example, "Monday-Friday 08:00 to 17:00 except public holidays". Service Hours should be defined in a *Service Level Agreement*.

Service Improvement Plan (SIP)
(Continual Service Improvement) A formal *Plan* to implement improvements to a *Process* or *IT Service*.

Service Knowledge Management System (SKMS)
(Service Transition) A set of tools and databases that are used to manage knowledge and information. The SKMS includes the *Configuration Management System*, as well as other tools and databases. The SKMS stores, manages, updates, and presents all information that an *IT Service Provider* needs to manage the full *Lifecycle* of *IT Services*.

Service Level
Measured and reported achievement against one or more *Service Level Targets*. The term Service Level is sometimes used informally to mean *Service Level Target*.

Service Level Agreement (SLA)

(Service Design) (Continual Service Improvement) An *Agreement* between an *IT Service Provider* and a *Customer*. The SLA describes the *IT Service*, documents *Service Level Targets*, and specifies the responsibilities of the *IT Service Provider* and the *Customer*. A single SLA may cover multiple *IT Services* or *multiple Customers*.
See **Operational Level Agreement.**

Service Level Management (SLM)

(Service Design) (Continual Service Improvement) The *Process* responsible for negotiating *Service Level Agreements*, and ensuring that these are met. SLM is responsible for ensuring that all *IT Service Management Processes*, *Operational Level Agreements*, and *Underpinning Contracts*, are appropriate for the agreed *Service Level Targets*. SLM monitors and reports on *Service Levels*, and holds regular *Customer reviews*.

Service Level Package (SLP)

(Service Strategy) A defined level of *Utility* and *Warranty* for a particular *Service Package*. Each SLP is designed to meet the needs of a *particular Pattern of Business Activity*.
See **Line of Service.**

Service Level Requirement (SLR)

(Service Design) (Continual Service Improvement) A *Customer Requirement* for an aspect of an *IT Service*. SLRs are based on *Business Objectives* and are used to negotiate agreed *Service Level Targets*.

Service Level Target

(Service Design) (Continual Service Improvement) A commitment that is documented in a *Service Level Agreement*. Service Level Targets are based on *Service Level Requirements*, and are needed to ensure that the *IT Service* design is *Fit for Purpose*. Service Level Targets should be *SMART*, and are usually based on *KPIs*.

Service Maintenance Objective

(Service Operation) The expected time that a *Configuration Item* will be unavailable due to planned maintenance *Activity*.

Service Management

A set of *Functions* and *Processes* for managing *Services* over their *Lifecycle*. Service Management is also used as a synonym for *IT Service Management*.

Service Management Lifecycle

An approach to *IT Service Management* that emphasises the importance of coordination and *Control* across the various *Functions, Processes,* and *Systems* necessary to manage the full *Lifecycle* of IT *Services*. The Service Management Lifecycle approach considers the *Strategy, Design, Transition, Operation* and *Continuous Improvement* of IT *Services*.

Service Manager

A manager who is responsible for managing the end-to-end *Lifecycle* of one or more *IT Services*. The term Service Manager is also used to mean any manager within the *IT Service Provider*. Most commonly used to refer to a *Business Relationship Manager*, a *Process Manager*, an *Account Manager* or a senior manager with responsibility for *IT Services* overall.

Service Operation

(Service Operation) A stage in the *Lifecycle* of an *IT Service*. Service Operation includes a number of *Processes* and *Functions* and is the title of one of the Core *ITIL* books.
See **Operation.**

Service Outage Analysis*

Synonym for *Service Failure Analysis (SFA)*.

Service Owner

(Continual Service Improvement) A *Role* which is accountable for the delivery of a specific *IT Service*.

Service Package

(Service Strategy) A detailed description of an *IT Service* that is available to be delivered to *Customers*. A Service Package includes a *Service Level Package* and one or more *Core Services* and *Supporting Services*.

Service Pipeline

(Service Strategy) A database or structured *Document* listing all *IT Services* that are under consideration or *Development*, but are not yet available to *Customers*. The Service Pipeline provides a *Business* view of possible future *IT Services* and is part of the *Service Portfolio* which is not normally published to *Customers*.

Service Portfolio

(Service Strategy) The complete set of *Services* that are managed by a *Service Provider*. The Service Portfolio is used to manage the entire *Lifecycle* of all *Services*, and includes three *Categories: Service Pipeline* (proposed or in *Development*); *Service Catalogue* (*Live* or available for *Deployment*); and *Retired Services*.

See **Service Portfolio Management, Contract Portfolio.**

Service Portfolio Management (SPM)

(Service Strategy) The *Process* responsible for managing the *Service Portfolio*. Service Portfolio Management considers *Services* in terms of the *Business* value that they provide.

Service Potential

(Service Strategy) The total possible value of the overall *Capabilities* and *Resources* of the *IT Service Provider*.

Service Provider

(Service Strategy) An *Organisation* supplying *Services* to one or more *Internal Customers* or *External Customers*. Service Provider is often used as an abbreviation for *IT Service Provider*.

See **Type I Service Provider, Type II Service Provider, Type III Service Provider.**

Service Provider Interface (SPI)

(Service Strategy) An interface between the *IT Service Provider* and a *User, Customer, Business Process,* or a *Supplier*. Analysis of Service Provider Interfaces helps to coordinate end-to-end management of *IT Services*.

Service Provisioning Optimization (SPO)

(Service Strategy) Analysing the finances and constraints of an *IT Service* to decide if alternative approaches to *Service* delivery might reduce *Costs* or improve *Quality*.

Service Reporting

(Continual Service Improvement) The *Process* responsible for producing and delivering reports of achievement and trends against *Service Levels*. Service Reporting should agree the format, content and frequency of reports with *Customers*.

Service Request

(Service Operation) A request from a *User* for information, or advice, or for a *Standard Change* or for *Access* to an *IT Service*. For example to reset a password, or to provide standard *IT Services* for a new *User*. Service Requests are usually handled by a *Service Desk*, and do not require an RFC to be submitted.

See **Request Fulfilment.**

Service Sourcing

(Service Strategy) The *Strategy* and approach for deciding whether to provide a *Service* internally or to *Outsource* it to an *External Service Provider*. Service Sourcing also means the execution of this *Strategy*.

Service Sourcing includes:

- *Internal Sourcing* - Internal or Shared Services using Type I or *Type II Service Providers*.
- Traditional Sourcing - Full Service Outsourcing using a *Type III Service Provider*.
- Multivendor Sourcing - Prime, Consortium or Selective Outsourcing using *Type III Service Providers*.

Service Strategy

(Service Strategy) The title of one of the Core *ITIL* books. Service Strategy establishes an overall *Strategy* for *IT Services* and for *IT Service Management*.

Service Transition

(Service Transition) A stage in the *Lifecycle* of an *IT Service*. Service Transition includes a number of *Processes* and *Functions* and is the title of one of the Core *ITIL* books.

See **Transition.**

Service Utility

(Service Strategy) The *Functionality* of an *IT Service* from the *Customer's* perspective. The *Business* value of an *IT Service* is created by the combination of Service Utility (what the Service does) and *Service Warranty* (how well it does it).

See **Utility.**

Service Validation and Testing

(Service Transition) The *Process* responsible for *Validation* and Testing of a new or *Changed IT Service*. Service Validation and Testing ensures that the *IT Service* matches its *Design Specification* and will meet the needs of the *Business*.

Service Valuation

(Service Strategy) A measurement of the total *Cost* of delivering an *IT Service*, and the total value to the *Business* of that IT Service. Service Valuation is used to help the *Business* and the *IT Service Provider* agree on the value of the *IT Service*.

Service Warranty

(Service Strategy) Assurance that an *IT Service* will meet agreed *Requirements*. This may be a formal *Agreement* such as a *Service Level Agreement* or *Contract*, or may be a marketing message or brand image. The *Business* value of an *IT Service* is created by the combination of *Service Utility* (what the Service does) and Service Warranty (how well it does it).
See **Warranty.**

Serviceability

(Service Design) (Continual Service Improvement) The ability of a *Third Party Supplier* to meet the terms of their *Contract*. This Contract will include agreed levels of *Reliability, Maintainability* or *Availability* for a *Configuration Item*.

Severity Code*

A *Category* used to represent Severity of a *Problem* or *Known Error*.
See **Impact Code.**

Shift

(Service Operation) A group or team of people who carry out a specific *Role* for a fixed period of time. For example there could be four shifts of *IT Operations Control* personnel to support an *IT Service* that is used 24 hours a day.

Simulation modelling

(Service Design) (Continual Service Improvement) A technique that creates a detailed *Model* to predict the behaviour of a *Configuration Item* or *IT Service*. Simulation Models can be very accurate but are expensive and time consuming to create. A Simulation Model is often created by using the actual *Configuration Items* that are being modelled, with artificial *Workloads* or *Transactions*. They are used in *Capacity Management* when accurate results are important. A simulation model is sometimes called a *Performance Benchmark*.

Single Point of Contact
(Service Operation) Providing a single consistent way to communicate with an *Organisation* or *Business Unit*. For example, a Single Point of Contact for an *IT Service Provider* is usually called a *Service Desk*.

Single Point of Failure (SPOF)
(Service Design) Any *Configuration Item* that can cause an *Incident* when it fails, and for which a *Countermeasure* has not been implemented. A SPOF may be a person, or a step in a *Process* or *Activity*, as well as a *Component* of the *IT Infrastructure*.
See **Failure.**

SLAM Chart
(Continual Service Improvement) A Service Level Agreement Monitoring Chart is used to help monitor and report achievements against *Service Level Targets*. A SLAM Chart is typically colour coded to show whether each agreed *Service Level Target* has been met, missed, or nearly missed during each of the previous 12 months.

SMART
(Service Design) (Continual Service Improvement) An acronym for helping to remember that targets in *Service Level Agreements* and *Project Plans* should be Specific, Measurable, Achievable, Relevant and Timely.

Snapshot
(Service Transition) The current state of a *Configuration* as captured by a discovery tool.
Also used as a synonym for *Benchmark*.
See **Baseline.**

Software Process Improvement and Capability dEtermination (SPICE)*
A framework for the assessment of software development processes, that evolved into ISO/IEC 15504. SPICE is partly based on the *Capability Maturity Model*.

Source
See **Service Sourcing.**

Spares Store*

One or more physical locations, set aside for the storage of hardware spares, maintained at the same level as *Configuration Items (CIs)* in the *Live Environment*.

Specification

A formal definition of *Requirements*. A Specification may be used to define technical or *Operational Requirements*, and may be internal or external. Many public *Standards* consist of a *Code of Practice* and a Specification. The Specification defines the *Standard* against which an *Organisation* can be *Audited*.

Stakeholder

All people who have an interest in an *Organisation, Project, IT Service* etc. Stakeholders may be interested in the *Activities*, targets, *Resources*, or *Deliverables*. Stakeholders may include *Customers, Partners*, employees, shareholders, owners, etc.
See **RACI.**

Standard

A mandatory Requirement. Examples include *ISO/IEC 20000* (an international Standard), an internal security Standard for Unix configuration, or a government Standard for how financial Records should be maintained. The term Standard is also used to refer to a *Code of Practice or Specification* published by a *Standards Organisation* such as *ISO* or *BSI*.
See **Guideline.**

Standard Change

(Service Transition) A pre-approved *Change* that is low *Risk*, relatively common and follows a *Procedure* or *Work Instruction*. For example password reset or provision of standard equipment to a new employee. *RFCs* are not required to implement a Standard Change, and they are logged and tracked using a different mechanism, such as a *Service Request*.
See **Change Model.**

Standard Operating Procedures (SOP)

(Service Operation) Procedures used by *IT Operations Management*.

Standby
(Service Design) Used to refer to *Resources* that are not required to deliver the *Live IT Services*, but are available to support *IT Service Continuity Plans*. For example a Standby data centre may be maintained to support *Hot Standby*, *Warm Standby* or *Cold Standby* arrangements.

Statement of requirements (SOR)
(Service Design) A *Document* containing all *Requirements* for a product purchase, or a new or changed *IT Service*.
See **Terms of Reference.**

Status
The name of a required field in many types of *Record*. It shows the current stage in the *Lifecycle* of the associated *Configuration Item*, *Incident*, *Problem* etc.

Status Accounting
(Service Transition) The *Activity* responsible for recording and reporting the *Lifecycle* of each *Configuration Item*.

Storage Management
(Service Operation) The *Process* responsible for managing the storage and maintenance of data throughout its *Lifecycle*.

Strategic
(Service Strategy) The highest of three levels of *Planning* and delivery (Strategic, *Tactical*, *Operational*). Strategic *Activities* include *Objective* setting and long term *Planning* to achieve the overall *Vision*.

Strategy
(Service Strategy) A *Strategic Plan* designed to achieve defined *Objectives*.

Super User
(Service Operation) A *User* who helps other *Users*, and assists in communication with the *Service Desk* or other parts of the *IT Service Provider*. Super Users typically provide support for minor *Incidents* and training.

Supplier
(Service Strategy) (Service Design) A *Third Party* responsible for supplying goods or *Services* that are required to deliver *IT services*. Examples of suppliers include commodity hardware and software vendors, network and telecom providers, and *Outsourcing Organisations*.
See **Underpinning Contract, Supply Chain.**

Supplier and Contract Database (SCD)
(Service Design) A database or structured *Document* used to manage *Supplier Contracts* throughout their *Lifecycle*. The SCD contains key *Attributes* of all *Contracts* with *Suppliers*, and should be part of the *Service Knowledge Management System*.

Supplier Management
(Service Design) The *Process* responsible for ensuring that all *Contracts* with *Suppliers* support the needs of the *Business*, and that all *Suppliers* meet their contractual commitments.

Supply Chain
(Service Strategy) The *Activities* in a *Value Chain* carried out by *Suppliers*. A Supply Chain typically involves multiple Suppliers, each adding value to the product or *Service*.
See **Value Network.**

Support Group
(Service Operation) A group of people with technical skills. Support Groups provide the *Technical Support* needed by all of the *IT Service Management Processes*.
See **Technical Management.**

Support Hours
(Service Design) (Service Operation) The times or hours when support is available to the *Users*. Typically this is the hours when the *Service Desk* is available. Support Hours should be defined in a *Service Level Agreement*, and may be different from *Service Hours*. For example, *Service Hours* may be 24 hours a day, but the Support Hours may be 07:00 to 19:00.

Supporting Service
(Service Strategy) A *Service* that enables or enhances a *Core Service*. For example a *Directory Service* or a *Backup Service*.
See **Service Package.**

SWOT Analysis

(Continual Service Improvement) A technique that reviews and analyses the internal strengths and weaknesses of an *Organisation* and the external opportunities and threats which it faces SWOT stands for Strengths, Weaknesses, Opportunities and Threats.

System

A number of related things that work together to achieve an overall *Objective*. For example:

- A computer System including hardware, software and *Applications*.
- A management System, including multiple *Processes* that are planned and managed together. For example a *Quality Management System*.
- A Database Management System or Operating System that includes many software modules that are designed to perform a set of related *Functions*.

System Management

The part of *IT Service Management* that focuses on the management of *IT Infrastructure* rather than *Process*.

Tactical
The middle of three levels of *Planning* and delivery (*Strategic*, Tactical, *Operational*). Tactical *Activities* include the medium term Plans required to achieve specific *Objectives*, typically over a period of weeks to months.

Tag
(Service Strategy) A short code used to identify a Category. For example tags EC1, EC2, EC3 etc. might be used to identify different *Customer* outcomes when analysing and comparing *Strategies*. The term Tag is also used to refer to the *Activity* of assigning Tags to things.

Task*
An *Activity* or set of activities that might be defined as part of a *Process*. Each Task should be documented in a *Procedure* or *Work Instruction*.

Technical Management
(Service Operation) The *Function* responsible for providing technical skills in support of *IT Services* and management of the *IT Infrastructure*. Technical Management defines the *Roles* of *Support Groups*, as well as the tools, *Processes* and *Procedures* required.

Technical Observation (TO)
(Continual Service Improvement) A technique used in *Service Improvement*, *Problem* investigation and *Availability Management*. Technical support staff meet to monitor the behaviour and *Performance* of an *IT Service* and make recommendations for improvement.

Technical Service
Synonym for *Infrastructure Service*.

Technical Severity*
Synonym for *Severity*.

Technical Support
Synonym for *Technical Management*.

Tension Metrics
(Continual Service Improvement) A set of related *Metrics*, in which improvements to one *Metric* have a negative effect on another. Tension Metrics are designed to ensure that an appropriate balance is achieved.

Terms of Reference (TOR)
(Service Design) A *Document* specifying the *Requirements, Scope, Deliverables, Resources* and schedule for a *Project* or *Activity*.

Test
(Service Transition) An *Activity* that verifies that a *Configuration Item, IT Service, Process*, etc. meets its *Specification* or agreed *Requirements*.
See **Service Validation and Testing, Acceptance.**

Test Environment
(Service Transition) A controlled *Environment* used to *Test Configuration Items, Builds, IT Services, Processes* etc.

Third Party
A person, group, or *Business* who is not part of the *Service Level Agreement* for an *IT Service*, but is required to ensure successful delivery of that *IT Service*. For example a software *Supplier*, a hardware maintenance company, or a facilities department. *Requirements* for Third Parties are typically specified in *Underpinning Contracts* or *Operational Level Agreements*.

Third-line Support
(Service Operation) The third level in a hierarchy of *Support Groups* involved in the resolution of *Incidents* and investigation of *Problems*. Each level contains more specialist skills, or has more time or other *Resources*.

Threat
Anything that might exploit a *Vulnerability*. Any potential cause of an *Incident* can be considered to be a Threat. For example a fire is a Threat that could exploit the *Vulnerability* of flammable floor coverings. This term is commonly used in *Information Security Management* and *IT Service Continuity Management*, but also applies to other areas such as *Problem* and *Availability Management*.

Threshold

The value of a *Metric* which should cause an *Alert* to be generated, or management action to be taken. For example "Priority1 Incident not solved within 4 hours", "more than 5 soft disk errors in an hour", or "more than 10 failed changes in a month".

Throughput

(Service Design) A measure of the number of *Transactions*, or other *Operations*, performed in a fixed time. For example 5000 emails sent per hour, or 200 disk I/Os per second.

Tied Users*

Users who have no choice other than to use the *IT Services* provided by their *Internal Service Provider*.
See **Untied Users.**

Total Cost of Ownership (TCO)

(Service Strategy) A methodology used to help make investment decisions. TCO assesses the full *Lifecycle Cost* of owning a *Configuration Item*, not just the initial *Cost* or purchase price.
See **Total Cost of Utilization.**

Total Cost of Utilization (TCU)

(Service Strategy) A methodology used to help make investment and *Service Sourcing* decisions. TCU assesses the full *Lifecycle Cost* to the *Customer* of using an *IT Service*.
See **Total Cost of Ownership.**

Total Quality Management (TQM)

(Continual Service Improvement) A methodology for managing continual Improvement by using a *Quality Management System*. TQM establishes a *Culture* involving all people in the *Organisation* in a *Process* of continual monitoring and improvement.

Transaction

A discrete *Function* performed by an *IT Service*. For example transferring money from one bank account to another. A single Transaction may involve numerous additions, deletions and modifications of data. Either all of these complete successfully or none of them is carried out.

Transition
(Service Transition) A change in state, corresponding to a movement of an *IT Service* or other *Configuration Item* from one *Lifecycle* status to the next.

Transition Planning and Support
(Service Transition) The *Process* responsible for Planning all *Service Transition Processes* and co-ordinating the resources that they require. These *Service Transition Processes* are *Change Management*, *Service Asset and Configuration Management*, *Release and Deployment Management*, *Service Validation and Testing*, *Evaluation*, and *Knowledge Management*.

Trend Analysis
(Continual Service Improvement) Analysis of data to identify time related patterns. Trend Analysis is used in *Problem Management* to identify common *Failures* or fragile *Configuration Items*, and in *Capacity Management* as a *Modelling* tool to predict future behaviour. It is also used as a management tool for identifying deficiencies in *IT Service Management Processes*.

Trouble Ticket*
A term used by some *Service Management* tools to refer to an *Incident*, a *Problem* or any other work item that can be assigned to support staff.

Tuning
The *Activity* responsible for *Planning Changes* to make the most efficient use of *Resources*. Tuning is part of *Performance Management*, which also includes *Performance Monitoring* and implementation of the required *Changes*.

Type I Service Provider
(Service Strategy) An *Internal Service Provider* that is embedded within a *Business Unit*. There may be several Type I Service Providers within an *Organisation*.

Type II Service Provider
(Service Strategy) An *Internal Service Provider* that provides shared *IT Services* to more than one *Business Unit*.

Type III Service Provider
(Service Strategy) A Service Provider that provides *IT Services* to *External Customers*.

Underpinning Contract (UC)

(Service Design) A *Contract* between an *IT Service Provider* and a *Third Party*. The *Third Party* provides goods or *Services* that support delivery of an *IT Service* to a *Customer*. The Underpinning Contract defines targets and responsibilities that are required to meet agreed *Service Level Targets* in an *SLA*.

Unit Cost

(Service Strategy) The *Cost* to the *IT Service Provider* of providing a single *Component* of an *IT Service*. For example the *Cost* of a single desktop PC, or of a single *Transaction*.

Untied Users*

Users who can choose whether to use the *Services* provided by an Internal *Service Provider* or to purchase services from another source.
See **Tied Users.**

Urgency

(Service Transition) (Service Design) A measure of how long it will be until an *Incident*, *Problem* or *Change* has a significant *Impact* on the *Business*. For example a high *Impact Incident* may have low Urgency, if the *Impact* will not affect the *Business* until the end of the financial year. *Impact* and Urgency are used to assign *Priority*.

Usability

(Service Design) The ease with which an *Application*, product, or *IT Service* can be used. Usability *Requirements* are often included in a *Statement of Requirements*.

Use Case

(Service Design) A technique used to define required functionality and *Objectives*, and to *Design Tests*. Use Cases define realistic scenarios that describe interactions between *Users* and an *IT Service* or other *System*.
See **Change Case.**

User

A person who uses the *IT Service* on a day-to-day basis. Users are distinct from *Customers*, as some *Customers* do not use the *IT Service* directly.

User Forum*

A formal meeting of *Users* that is usually organised by the *Service Provider* to measure satisfaction and to gain feedback to help with *Continual Improvement*.

User Profile (UP)

(Service Strategy) A pattern of *User* demand for *IT Services*. Each User Profile includes one or more *Patterns* of *Business Activity*.

Utility

(Service Strategy) Functionality offered by a *Product* or *Service* to meet a particular need. Utility is often summarised as "what it does".
See **Service Utility.**

Validation

(Service Transition) An *Activity* that ensures a new or changed *IT Service, Process, Plan*, or other *Deliverable* meets the needs of the *Business*. Validation ensures that *Business Requirements* are met even though these may have changed since the original Design.

See **Verification, Acceptance, Qualification, Service Validation and Testing.**

Value Chain

(Service Strategy) A sequence of *Processes* that creates a product or *Service* that is of value to a *Customer*. Each step of the sequence builds on the previous steps and contributes to the overall product or *Service*.

See **Value Network.**

Value for Money

An informal measure of *Cost Effectiveness*. Value for Money is often based on a comparison with the Cost of alternatives.

See **Cost Benefit Analysis.**

Value Network

(Service Strategy) A complex set of *Relationships* between two or more groups or organisations. Value is generated through exchange of knowledge, information, goods or Services.

See **Value Chain, Partnership.**

Value on Investment (VOI)

(Continual Service Improvement) A measurement of the expected benefit of an investment. VOI considers both financial and intangible benefits.

See **Return on Investment.**

Variable Cost

(Service Strategy) A *Cost* that depends on how much the *IT Service* is used, how many products are produced, the number and type of *Users*, or something else that cannot be fixed in advance.

See **Variable Cost Dynamics.**

Variable Cost Dynamics

(Service Strategy) A technique used to understand how overall *Costs* are impacted by the many complex variable elements that contribute to the provision of *IT Services*.

Variance

The difference between a planned value and the actual measured value. Commonly used in *Financial Management*, *Capacity Management* and *Service Level Management*, but could apply in any area where *Plans* are in place.

Verification

(Service Transition) An *Activity* that ensures a new or changed *IT Service*, *Process*, *Plan*, or other *Deliverable* is complete, accurate, *Reliable* and matches its *Design Specification*.

See **Validation, Acceptance, Service Validation and Testing.**

Verification and Audit

(Service Transition) The *Activities* responsible for ensuring that information in the *CMDB* is accurate and that all *Configuration Items* have been identified and recorded in the CMDB. Verification includes routine checks that are part of other *Processes*. For example, verifying the serial number of a desktop PC when a *User* logs an *Incident*. *Audit* is a periodic, formal check.

Version

(Service Transition) A Version is used to identify a specific *Baseline* of a *Configuration Item*. Versions typically use a naming convention that enables the sequence or date of each *Baseline* to be identified. For example Payroll Application Version 3 contains updated functionality from Version 2.

Vision

A description of what the *Organisation* intends to become in the future. A Vision is created by senior management and is used to help influence *Culture* and *Strategic Planning*.

Vital Business Function (VBF)

(Service Design) A *Function* of a *Business Process* which is critical to the success of the *Business*. Vital Business Functions are an important consideration of *Business Continuity Management*, *IT Service Continuity Management* and *Availability Management*.

Vulnerability

A weakness that could be exploited by a *Threat*. For example an open firewall port, a password that is never changed, or a flammable carpet. A missing *Control* is also considered to be a Vulnerability.

Warm Standby
Synonym for *Intermediate Recovery*.

Warranty
(Service Strategy) A promise or guarantee that a product or *Service* will meet its agreed *Requirements*.
See **Service Validation and Testing, Service Warranty.**

Waterline*
A way of presenting the *Service Catalogue*. *Business Services* are made visible to the *Customer* and are considered to be above the waterline, *Technical Services* are not made visible and are considered to be below the waterline. This metaphor is based on the fact that the parts of an ocean liner below the waterline are the engines and propulsion system, and these are not normally visible to passengers.

Work in Progress (WIP)
A *Status* that means *Activities* have started but are not yet complete. It is commonly used as a *Status* for *Incidents, Problems, Changes* etc.

Work Instruction
A *Document* containing detailed instructions that specify exactly what steps to follow to carry out an *Activity*. A Work Instruction contains much more detail than a *Procedure* and is only created if very detailed instructions are needed.

Workaround
(Service Operation) Reducing or eliminating the *Impact* of an *Incident* or *Problem* for which a full *Resolution* is not yet available. For example by restarting a failed *Configuration Item*. Workarounds for *Problems* are documented in *Known Error Records*. Workarounds for *Incidents* that do not have associated *Problem Records* are documented in the *Incident Record*.

Workflow Diagram*
A diagram that represents a *Process* or *Activity*. Workflow Diagrams show steps, timings and exchanges of information with other *Processes* or *Activities*.

Workload

The *Resources* required to deliver an identifiable part of an *IT Service*. Workloads may be *Categorised* by *Users*, groups of *Users*, or *Functions* within the *IT Service*. This is used to assist in analysing and managing the *Capacity*, *Performance* and *Utilisation* of *Configuration Items* and *IT Services*. The term Workload is sometimes used as a synonym for *Throughput*.

Workload Management*

Activities in *Capacity Management* that predict *Workload* trends and analyse their likely effects.

ACD	Automatic Call Distribution
AM	Availability Management
AMIS	Availability Management Information System
ASP	Application Service Provider
BCM	Business Capacity Management
BCM	Business Continuity Management
BCP	Business Continuity Plan
BIA	Business Impact Analysis
BRM	Business Relationship Manager
BSI	British Standards Institution
BSM	Business Service Management
CAB	Change Advisory Board
CAB/EC	Change Advisory Board / Emergency Committee
CAPEX	Capital Expenditure
CCM	Component Capacity Management
CFIA	Component Failure Impact Analysis
CI	Configuration Item
CMDB	Configuration Management Database
CMIS	Capacity Management Information System
CMM	Capability Maturity Model
CMMI	Capability Maturity Model Integration
CMS	Configuration Management System
COTS	Commercial off the Shelf
CSF	Critical Success Factor
CSI	Continual Service Improvement
CSIP	Continual Service Improvement Programme
CSP	Core Service Package
CTI	Computer Telephony Integration
DIKW	Data-to-Information-to-Knowledge-to-Wisdom
eSCM-CL	eSourcing Capability Model for Client Organizations
eSCM-SP	eSourcing Capability Model for Service Providers
FMEA	Failure Modes and Effects Analysis
FTA	Fault Tree Analysis
IRR	Internal Rate of Return
ISG	IT Steering Group

ISM	Information Security Management
ISMS	Information Security Management System
ISO	International Organization for Standardization
ISP	Internet Service Provider
IT	Information Technology
ITSCM	IT Service Continuity Management
ITSM	IT Service Management
itSMF	IT Service Management Forum
IVR	Interactive Voice Response
KEDB	Known Error Database
KPI	Key Performance Indicator
LOS	Line of Service
MoR	Management of Risk
MTBF	Mean Time Between Failures
MTBSI	Mean Time Between Service Incidents
MTRS	Mean Time to Restore Service
MTTR	Mean Time to Repair
NPV	Net Present Value
OGC	Office of Government Commerce
OLA	Operational Level Agreement
OPEX	Operational Expenditure
OPSI	Office of Public Sector Information
PBA	Pattern of Business Activity
PFS	Prerequisite for Success
PIR	Post Implementation Review
PSA	Projected Service Availability
QA	Quality Assurance
QMS	Quality Management System
RCA	Root Cause Analysis
RFC	Request for Change
ROI	Return on Investment
RPO	Recovery Point Objective
RTO	Recovery Time Objective
SAC	Service Acceptance Criteria
SACM	Service Asset and Configuration Management
SCD	Supplier and Contract Database
SCM	Service Capacity Management
SFA	Service Failure Analysis
SIP	Service Improvement Plan
SKMS	Service Knowledge Management System
SLA	Service Level Agreement

SLM	Service Level Management
SLP	Service Level Package
SLR	Service Level Requirement
SMO	Service Maintenance Objective
SoC	Separation of Concerns
SOP	Standard Operating Procedures
SOR	Statement of requirements
SPI	Service Provider Interface
SPM	Service Portfolio Management
SPO	Service Provisioning Optimization
SPOF	Single Point of Failure
TCO	Total Cost of Ownership
TCU	Total Cost of Utilization
TO	Technical Observation
TOR	Terms of Reference
TQM	Total Quality Management
UC	Underpinning Contract
UP	User Profile
VBF	Vital Business Function
VOI	Value on Investment
WIP	Work in Progress

Further Guidance and Contact Points

itSMF Ltd.
150 Wharfedale Road
Winnersh Triangle
Wokingham
Berkshire RG41 5RB
United Kingdom
Tel: +44(0)118 918 6500
Fax: +44(0)118 969 9749
E-mail: service@itsmf.co.uk
www.itsmf.co.uk

TSO
PO Box 29
Norwich NR3 1GN
United Kingdom
Tel: +44(0) 870 600 5522
Fax: +44(0) 870 600 5533
E-mail: customer.services@tso.co.uk
www.tso.co.uk

British Standards Institution
389 Chiswick High Road
London W4 4AL
United Kingdom
Tel: +44(0)208 996 9001
Fax: +44(0)208 996 7001
E-mail: info@bsi-global.com
www.bsi-global.com

OGC
Rosebery Court
St Andrews Business Park
Norwich NR7 0HS
United Kingdom
Tel: +44(0)1603 704567
Fax: +44(0)1603 704817
E-mail: info@ogc.gov.uk
www.ogc.gov.uk
www.itil.co.uk

APM Group Limited
Sword House
Totteridge Road
High Wycombe
Buckinghamshire
HP13 6DG
Tel: +44 (0) 1494 452 450
Fax: +44 (0) 1494 459 559
Email:servicedesk@apmgroup.co.uk
www.apmgroup.co.uk

About itSMF

The itSMF is the only truly independent and internationally recognised forum for IT Service Management professionals worldwide. This not-for-profit organisation is a prominent player in the on-going development and promotion of IT Service Management "best practice", standards and qualifications and has been since 1991.

Globally, the itSMF now boasts over 6000 member companies, blue chip and public sector alike, covering in excess of 70,000 individuals spread over 40+ international Chapters.

Each chapter is a separate legal entity and is largely autonomous. The UK Chapter has over 16,000 members: it offers a flourishing annual conference, online bookstore, regular regional meetings and special interest groups and numerous other benefits for members. Its website is at www.itsmf.co.uk.

There is a separate International entity that provides an overall steering and support function to existing and emerging chapters. It has its own website at **www.itsmf.org.**